Inscribing the Text

John O. Powell

Inscribing the Text

Sermons and Prayers of Walter Brueggemann

Edited by Anna Carter Florence

FORTRESS PRESS / MINNEAPOLIS

INSCRIBING THE TEXT
Sermons and Prayers of Walter Brueggemann

Cover image: Detail from the *Madonna of the Magnificat* by Sandro Botticelli (1445–1510). ©Archivo Iconografico, S.A./CORBIS. c.1480–1481. Tempera on panel. Galleria degli Uffizi, Florence, Italy. Used by permission.
    The full painting shows Mary with the infant Jesus on her lap surrounded by angels. Mary's hand is dipping a pen into an inkwell as if she is about to inscribe words on the page, while Jesus' hand is pointing to the words already inscribed in the Magnificat in Luke 1:46-55.

Jacket and book design: Zan Ceeley

ISBN 0-8006-3646-5

The paper used in this publication meets the minimum requirements of American National Standard for Information Sciences — Permanence of Paper for Printed Library Materials, ANSI Z329.48-1984.

Printed in Canada

09   08   07   06   05   2   3   4   5   6   7   8   9

In Memory of August L. Brueggemann

In Expectation for Emilia Mary Brueggemann

Contents

Editor's Foreword

In at least one respect, preaching students are not so different from acting students. They don't begin with the text. They begin with imitation.

Hand a fledgling actor a scene from *A Streetcar Named Desire*, tell him you want him to read the part of Stanley, and brace yourself, because any moment Marlon Brando is going to come charging into the room. Give a budding actress the score to *Sweeney Todd*, ask her to sing through it, and what you will hear is her best impersonation of Angela Lansbury. This is inevitable; it is also, frankly, a little tiring for teachers and can make for a dreary few weeks at the start of the term. Teachers understand, however, that this is part of the process: beginning students do not play the scene that is written; they imitate the actors they admire. If they want to act, they have to learn the difference between interpretation and imitation. They have to peel back the layers of caricature until they encounter the text.

I can always tell when my students have been listening to Walter Brueggemann, because I begin to feel like Judi Dench and Robert DeNiro have invaded my classroom. The students don't step into the pulpit; they grab it. They don't open their Bibles; they snap them. Shoulders hunched, eyebrows arched, they growl and glare and toss their heads like lions. Their scripture readings sound like a cross between a live radio sportscast and the Queen's annual Christmas address. There are trios of adjectives and torrents of verbs. It is hard to make it to the end of this kind of sermon with a straight face, but I know the students do not mean to be funny. They are sincere. Brueggemann is one of their preaching heroes, and they are looking for role models. My job is to gently pull them back to the task at hand without taking all the wind out of their sails. I am sure, I tell them, that Dr. Brueggemann would be flattered by how closely you have been paying attention to him, and, yes, he is an extraordinary and incomparable preacher; but don't confuse preaching like him with imitating him. If you want to preach like Brueggemann, don't copy his mannerisms. Follow his example. Preach the text.

This volume contains the most recent collection of Walter Brueggemann's sermons and prayers. That would be notable in itself: another dazzling set of words from a man whose sheer energy and creativity make us wonder if he is climbing Sinai every morning, for dictation. Yet this book is more than a collection. The opening article lifts up a startling new metaphor for preacher: that of *scribe*. Adapted from a lecture Brueggemann delivered at the Festival of Preaching in 2002, this relatively short piece distills years of textual study—so much of it in direct service to proclamation—into a concise homiletic that proposes a radical shift in the way we think about and embody the act of preaching.

Students and readers of Brueggemann will hear cadences of familiar themes: in the scribe, we hear poet and prophet, testimony and resistance, truth and power, exile and captivity. The scribe's work is repetitive and rhythmic: to stand up, week after week, and offer texts to people who can't remember their own story for longer than five minutes, people who have bought into a fiction of power and money and scarcity of resources. Text after text, week after week. On the surface it doesn't look like much. But this work of inscribing is how one re-texts a community with God's truth, and the scribe trusts that it is enough; the *texts* are enough. Grass withers, flowers fade, but texts linger; they de-center; they explode. Inscribe the text, and it ignites fireworks of alternative imagination. Preach the text, and it sets the people on fire.

Brueggemann's homiletic of the scribe is, in my view, a landmark in the field. It stands with Karl Barth's *Homiletics* as another brief but passionate call for the strange, new world of the biblical text to have its say, as free as possible from the preacher's reductive instincts to embroider and protect. And that is no surprise: Brueggemann, like Barth before him, has devoted a lifetime to the study of word and text *for preachers*. His ideas, like Barth's, remain big enough, expansive enough, to open up or join conversations far beyond his own context—or even the contexts of those who would harden the words in opaque orthodoxies. In time, I believe, we will look back over the last century and see the work of these two scholars—one a systematic theologian, the other a biblical theologian—as having made the most important, the most enduring, and indeed the most generative contributions to the act of preaching than any others we might name. The scribe may indeed be a Sinai-inspired and Sinai-inscribed homiletic. And the sermons and prayers of this particular scribe—though in this form they can only be read, not experienced—will linger to re-text and re-ignite another generation of preachers.

ANNA CARTER FLORENCE
COLUMBIA THEOLOGICAL SEMINARY

Acknowledgments

I am glad to record my thanks to my colleague Anna Carter Florence, who worked mightily to transpose my sermons into this book. It is clear to me that she and I are on the same page about preaching, and that encourages me greatly. I am also grateful to Tia Foley, who has the uncommon gift of turning my random words into manuscript pages that permit my preaching. My thanks to K. C. Hanson, Zan Ceeley, and the other good people at Fortress Press is deep and abiding.

I am glad to dedicate this book to my father, August Brueggemann, and to my youngest grandchild, Emilia Mary Brueggemann. My father, as my teacher and pastor, was the first and primary one who inscribed the text on my heart. My granddaughter awaits such inscription. He would have wanted that for her.

Walter Brueggemann
Ascension Day 2003

Inscribing the Text

On Generosity

On our own, we conclude:
that there is not enough to go around
we are going to run short
       of money
       of love
       of grades
       of publications
       of sex
       of beer
       of members
       of years
       of life
we should seize the day
       seize the goods
       seize our neighbor's goods
because there is not enough to go around.

And in the midst of our perceived deficit:
       You come
       You come giving bread in the wilderness
       You come giving children at the 11th hour
       You come giving homes to exiles
       You come giving futures to the shut-down
       You come giving Easter joy to the dead
       You come—fleshed in Jesus.

And we watch while
       the blind receive their sight
       the lame walk
       the lepers are cleansed

the deaf hear
the dead are raised
the poor dance and sing.

We watch
        and we take food we did not grow and
            life we did not invent and
            future that is gift and gift and gift and
            families and neighbors who sustain us
                        when we do not deserve it.

It dawns on us—late rather than soon—
        that "you give food in due season
        you open your hand
                    and satisfy the desire of every living thing."

By your giving, break our cycles of imagined scarcity
            override our presumed deficits
            quiet our anxieties of lack
            transform our perceptual field to see
                        the abundance . . . mercy upon mercy
                                    blessing upon blessing.

Sink your generosity deep into our lives
        that your muchness may expose our false lack
        that endlessly receiving, we may endlessly give,
            so that the world may be made Easter new,
            without greedy lack, but only *wonder*
            without coercive need, but only *love*
            without destructive greed, but only *praise*
            without aggression and invasiveness . . .
                all things Easter new . . .
                    all around us, toward us and
                                by us
                all things Easter new.

Finish your creation . . . in *wonder, love,* and *praise.* Amen.

Columbia Theological Seminary chapel service / September 26, 2002

The Preacher as Scribe

L et me begin by considering four scriptural confrontations that
might construe preaching as *truth speaking to power*. In these
classic texts, the "hero," the one with whom we side in the narrative,
is the *preacher,* the one who has been authorized by call to utter truth
that lies outside the horizon of those addressed. His preaching aims
to assure by an alternative and to jar by exposé. It compels and impels
action in a new direction. It is hard work—and no wonder.

I

The primal case of speaking-truth-to-power in the Old Testament is
Moses addressing Pharaoh. As a truth-teller, Moses had as long a
preparation for his call as any of us. He was birthed in danger because
Pharaoh, the quintessence of power, had already generically decreed
his death as a baby. He was schooled as a freedom fighter (read *terrorist*) and, like his fellow Hebrews, resented the Egyptian adminis-
trators—so resented, in fact, that he killed an Egyptian. For his
moment of rage, Moses became a fugitive and was forced to flee the
empire. And it was in his status as a fugitive that he was addressed by
this voice from the burning bush who summons, authorizes, and dispatches him to Pharaoh.

Moses can think of at least four reasons *not* to undertake such a
risky venture as speaking-truth-to-power: (1) he is inadequate; (2)
they will want to know who the God is who sends; (3) they will not
believe; (4) he can't talk right. When his reasoning makes no difference, he resorts to begging: Send someone else! But the one who calls
and voices truth will not be put off. Truth must be uttered, and finally,
in chapter 5, it is: *Thus says the LORD, the God of Israel: let my people
go, so that they may celebrate a festival to me in the wilderness.*

The truth Moses utters is the truth of YHWH: Pharaoh is penultimate and accountable to YHWH, and YHWH, not Pharaoh, must be

glorified and obeyed. The familiar "Let my people go" is in fact an imperative—*Send my people!*—which YHWH issues through Moses. The king of Egypt is hardly accustomed to hearing imperatives spoken to him, but the truth is that *he* is out of business. YHWH is sovereign and the power of Pharaoh is dissolved. As a consequence and by-product, Israel is emancipated. *That* is the truth, the truth of YHWH; it is, moreover, the disastrous truth of Pharaoh. It took Moses—frightened, mumbling Moses—to engage in proclamation that changed history and founded the missional people of God in the world.

A second familiar case study of speaking-truth-to-power is *Nathan addressing David* (2 Samuel 12). We know all about David, the giant-killing boy, the man's man; his rise to power is an amazing saga. Born to privilege, he quickly surpasses his seven older siblings in favor and is anointed king and Messiah while still a youth. David is soldier, chief, intimidator; everything happens well for him. Women adore him. Men trust and admire him. Very few people are able to say *No* to him, and the ones who do, die like flies. Indeed, David is the beneficiary of many convenient deaths—so many, in fact, that he is endlessly under suspicion.

So David arrives in power after a long winning streak. He is king in Hebron for seven years, then promoted to Jerusalem, where he is settled, safe, prosperous . . . *bored*. He is so bored that he seeks diversion and spots it in Bathsheba. She, like everyone before her, does not resist him; the rest, as they say, is history—but what a history. *Cover-up. Murder.* Everything is done in the interest of protecting this king who is above the Torah, who has no restraints, who will have what he wants, who bends the whole world to his whim.

Enter Nathan, the prophet on the payroll of the king; enter truth! Back in chapter 7, Nathan had given divine oracle to David in the form of a blank check from God: *But I will not take my steadfast love from him, as I took it from Saul, whom I put away from before you. Your house and your kingdom shall be made sure forever before me; your throne shall be established forever* (2 Sam 7:15-16). That word of truth had been a fairly easy one for the prophet to utter, but in the wake of the scandal with Bathsheba and Uriah, Nathan has a more demanding assignment. He must still tell the truth, the truth from the same God to the same king. But since the God of the wondrous *royal oracle* of 2 Samuel 7 is also the God of the *sturdy Torah,* this time around it will be far more dangerous. How is one to communicate to this king who has known no restraint that there is an intransigent restraint in the Torah that *cannot* be violated?

The prophet Nathan wisely resorts to a figure of speech, a parable. He employs an artistic euphemism to soften the truth, hoping to divert the king's attention until the connection is made. He tells a story about a rich man with many sheep and a poor man with one sheep. David gets the point and expresses his indignation, unwittingly condemning his own royal action: *Then David's anger was greatly kindled against the man. He said to Nathan, "As the LORD lives, the man who has done this deserves to die; he shall restore the lamb fourfold, because he did this thing, and because he had no pity"* (2 Sam 12:5-6). So far, so good: the ploy is working. Now it is up to the truth-teller to close the deal by unmasking the king. It takes only two words: *attah ha'ish* ("You are the man!").[1] Just two words, but what courage to say them! What risk! In these two words, everything is at stake for Nathan: his office, his prestige, his future, his wealth. And he *must* say them. He must deconstruct royal self-regard in order to assert that before the intransigence of the Torah, the king stands exposed and equal to every other Israelite: *nothing special, no exception*—and it has been forever since anyone has risked telling David *that*.

It belongs to David's magnificence that in this dangerous moment he responds to Nathan's parable as a son of the Torah. He utters two words of his own: *"ḥaṭa'ti YHWH"* ("I have sinned against the LORD"). Power repents. The truth prevails. It is the way such encounters are supposed to work, and what a relief for Nathan, who had no clue when he risked life and future that *his* encounter with power would go so well. Very often, power does not yield to truth. This time, however, it does, and ever since, preachers who must speak-truth-to-power have followed Nathan's rhetorical example by employing "illustrations."

The third well-known case of speaking-truth-to-power is *Elijah addressing Ahab* in the story of Naboth's vineyard (1 Kings 21). Like the modern day cases of Watergate and Whitewater and Enron, the narrative turns on an inconspicuous deal that of itself amounts to nothing, yet quickly escalates into a great affair of state—and a royal mess. In this case, the story begins with a modest real estate deal: Ahab wants a tract of land owned by Naboth for his vegetable garden. The king offers to pay, because he assumes, in good Baalistic fashion, that everything and everyone is a purchasable commodity. He is

7

stunned when Naboth, a powerless Israelite, refuses the request of the king in a remarkable act of resistance: *But Naboth said to Ahab, "The LORD forbid that I should give you my ancestral inheritance"* (1 Kgs 21:3). Ahab is defeated. He goes home, takes to his bed, and sulks.

The story *would* end there, except for Ahab's wife, the queen Jezebel. She is not a native-born Israelite, not a child of Torah, not subject to old tribal restraints: *she* knows how to move in the world . . . and she moves. Jezebel scolds her husband for giving up so easily, and makes him a promise: *Do you now govern Israel? Get up, eat some food, and be cheerful; I will give you the vineyard of Naboth the Jezreelite* (1 Kgs 21:7). She orchestrates a judicial scenario against the innocent Naboth, frames him, and gets him stoned as an enemy of God and state. As soon as Ahab hears that Naboth is dead, he scuttles over to the vineyard to take possession of it. Land acquired, crown vindicated, case closed.

The story *should* end there, except for the prophet Elijah. Elijah has been previously introduced as a dangerous guy who eats no royal junk food and lives on brook water and supplies flown in by bird. He is completely outside the system, and he has no interest in exhibiting "pastoral presence." As God's truth-teller, Elijah swoops down on Ahab with an incredibly harsh oracle of punishment: for having done evil in the sight of the Lord, Ahab and his entire dynasty will be consumed and cut off; for having instigated murder and dispossession, Jezebel shall be eaten by dogs. The truth told here is as sweeping as it is breathtaking, leaving no exception to death: every male in Israel, slave or free, shall die. The severity of God's indictment and sentence may seem disproportionate for seizing one vegetable garden and killing one small farmer, but of course, Naboth is one of *many* so violated. Naboth is only an instant in a general policy of ruthless royal acquisitiveness, and the God of Torah, concretized in Naboth, will not tolerate it. It is the truth, the truth given by Elijah: YHWH will not be mocked by power. And while Elijah is fearless in uttering this truth before the king, we should not gloss over the risk.

The fourth case of truth-speaking-to-power is *Daniel addressing Nebuchadnezzar* (Daniel 4). Nebuchadnezzar is the king of Babylon, and even more than Pharaoh before him, he is the quintessential symbol for extreme power in the Old Testament. Yet it seems that this king of everything has had a terrible nightmare, the kind we have when we are anxious or uneasy about our power. He summons his entire research and development cadre, but dreams are secret, night-time messages from God that lie outside the scope of technocrats, and none can interpret it. Desperate to learn the truth of his nightmare, Nebuchadnezzar finally calls for Daniel, who is known to be peculiarly endowed with hermeneutical skills. The king, so the story goes, has confidence in this Jew with extraordinary gifts of wisdom, and he reiterates his dream to Daniel. It is a remarkable act of vulnerability—for extreme power to place itself in a position of deference before truth.

Daniel hears the dream and knows its meaning immediately. But as the text says, he is severely distressed and his thoughts terrify him, because the news for Nebuchadnezzar is not good. Daniel trembles to think of what may happen to him if he relays the message; the risk of interpretation is frighteningly high. The king reassures and pleads, however, and finally Daniel tells him the meaning of his dream: Nebuchadnezzar will be severely demoted from his glorious power and driven away from human society to dwell among wild animals. And he will remain in this sorry and humiliating state, Daniel says, . . . *until you have learned that the Most High has sovereignty over the kingdom of mortals and gives it to whom he will* (4:20). Isn't that the same lesson truth must *always* speak to power? The word of the dream, which is itself beyond royal control, is that power invested in human agents is *never* ultimate.

Daniel goes on to advise the king that he atone for his sins with righteousness, but as far as we know, the counsel goes unheeded. So we are not surprised to learn that the dream comes to reality, just as Daniel said: the king and his power are deconstructed. Nebuchadnezzar becomes like an animal that eats grass, grows long hair, and has nails like claws. He is utterly ungroomed, and his being so is a sign of powerlessness: by the hidden sovereignty of God, Nebuchadnezzar is *un-created*. He is less, now, than the creature God had first made him to be. It is exactly as Daniel the truth-teller had seen and announced.

The astonishing thing about this narrative is that it does not end there, as we might expect; it continues full circle, until deconstruction turns to restoration. Amazingly enough, Nebuchadnezzar recovers his sanity. And in his sanity, he does the sanest thing imaginable: he sings doxology to the Most High, a public, lyrical act of ceding ultimate authority out beyond himself. Having been addressed by truth, this man of power is *re-created*. He no longer imagines his power to be ultimate. Instead, he knows, decisively, that it is penultimate, and to be marked by practices of truth, justice, and lowliness. This was not possible before doxology, and the doxology was not possible until he heard the truth. The dream of the night has subverted the illusion of the day.

II

These are four cases of truth-speaking-to-power. We could cite many others in scripture and beyond, and it might be enough to say to those who preach, "Go and do likewise." But I have cited these four cases precisely because I want to consider the challenge of that crisp model of preaching. *There are deeply problematic things about the model of truth-speaking-to-power.*

The fact is that truth-speaking-to-power is a simple and perhaps simplistic model that almost none of us can readily embrace. When we preside over institutions with programs, budgets, and anxiety-filled members, we are not likely to practice, with any simplicity at all, the notion of truth-speaking-to-power—not if we want to keep our jobs. Certainly there are occasional dramatic moments when truth can and must be spoken directly to power. But on the whole, the model of truth-speaking-to-power is not possible in our society, particularly in local congregations where one is cast as preacher *and* administrator. It is utterly impossible to be charged with both truth-telling and maintenance.

Perhaps only the tenured, the independently wealthy, or those at the end of a career can afford to speak-truth-to-power. Perhaps only the fugitive, the raven-fed, the royally paid, or the clairvoyant among us will be brave enough and detached enough to speak at all. Perhaps we *are* too well-kept; perhaps security drains us of courage. But does our context afford us any alternatives? Very few of us seem destined to speak-truth-to-power so clearly that it will dismantle an empire and free slaves. Very few of us are likely to crash the palace and tell an incriminating story. Very few of us will announce the king's death sentence or interpret royal dreams. It simply doesn't come up.

Beyond these harsh realities, however, there are other reasons that truth-speaking-to-power is problematic. Notions of *truth* and *power* are now situated in a postmodern world, and easy assumptions of authority are profoundly precarious. First, consider *power*. It is clear enough to identify in the four scriptural cases: power is *Pharaoh*. Power is *the king*. But in our complex world of interlocking systems, power is less clear. It is endlessly subtle and elusive, shifting and restless. We cannot easily identify it. Those who are clearly linked with power (executives of large corporations, for instance) may describe themselves as relatively powerless in the larger capitalist system. Moreover, the pastoral task is primarily one of *empowerment*—that is, instilling in others the readiness to accept and affirm what power there is, or could be, had we courage to embrace a different notion of power, a different perspective of ourselves in the world. Such a task requires us to move beyond flat definitions of power, and it is difficult work, indeed.

Conversely, consider *truth*. There was a time when the authority of the church and the authority of the preacher were immense. There was a time when the preacher was the best-educated "man" in town. There was a time when issues were less complex, or seemed to be—but not now. Truth in our day has become democratized and secularized. It is held in many quarters. We may easily confess it—the claim of the sovereignty of the triune God, for instance—but we less easily proclaim it. We may quickly locate it—with pain and suffering and the Friday cross, for example—but we cannot claim a monopoly on it. We may readily believe it—that Gospel truth is transformative and emancipatory in human lives—but we strain to define or enact it. In a postmodern world, both *truth* and *power* are complex and evasive, and we cannot easily assume our own certitude or importance. We cannot automatically cast ourselves as Moses or Nathan or Elijah or Daniel, no matter how endlessly we are tempted. Besides, if we are casting to type, it may be that we fit the part of the royally and sinfully acquisitive, rather than the truth-teller.

III

Speaking-truth-to-power is indeed problematic for us. Yet just because it is hard to render these texts of confrontation, it does not follow that they are useless for us, or that we need to find more palatable texts. Rather, I want to insist that these confrontational scenarios are . . . *texts*.

This may sound obvious to you, but notice that almost all of us are schooled in historical criticism, either directly (pastors) or by osmosis (lay people). What we *know* how to do, what we *want* to do, is to *go behind the text* to the drama of real life that we can then reenact. What we have in the Bible, however, is not real-life historical drama.

What we have is a *text* that stands some distance removed from whatever historical encounter *might* have happened.

To say the Bible is a *text* means:

- that it stands some distance from the reality of raw facticity,
- that it is a stylized, artistic act of imagination,
- that the act of imagination has transposed history into artistry,
- that this artistic transposition from factual happening (to which we have no access) to text (which we have in our hands) is accomplished by the imaginative work of real agents who intentionally make text.

While there are many things we do not know about how and when the Bible was written, we do know that the text was most likely composed in the sixth, fifth, and fourth centuries B.C.E. That is when the artistic imagination of the writers firmed into narrative text. And this time of text-making was a time when Israel had no more kings and very few prophets. All that was left as a driving force for Judaism were *scribes*. The text, therefore, consists of *remembered* confrontations between power (kings) and truth (prophets) given to us through *scribal refraction*—that is, through an intentional, self-conscious, interpretative editorial process. This is a vastly different approach to the text from that of historical criticism, but it is the direction in which current scholarship is rapidly going. I suggest that *scribal refraction* is important not only for understanding the text, but also for *preaching,* if the simple model of speaking-truth-to-power no longer holds for us.

Most of us think of scribes as part of the "Pharisees and hypocrites" crowd, but that is a misleading stereotype from New Testament polemics. I want to speak a good word for scribes. They are actually the school-men, the book-men, and the scroll-makers who gathered old traditions and memories and preserved them in text form. Some of the best-known scribes are *Baruch,* who created some form of the book of Jeremiah; Baruch's brother, *Seraiah,* who also wrote for Jeremiah; and *Ezra,* the quintessential scribe, who is largely responsible for making Judaism into a community of text practice. In Ezra's day, the Jewish people had been tossed about by the vagaries of historical circumstance and had largely forgotten their theological identity in the rootage of Moses. What Ezra did was to *re-text* this community: to turn the imagination and the practice of the Jewish people back to their most elemental assurances and claims. And from this re-texting effort, three things evolved: the canon, the community of Judaism, and the distinctive practice of lively, generative textual interpretation, which marks rabbinic teaching and the identity of Judaism even to this day.

Ezra's context is very like our own. Preaching in postmodern North America addresses folks of Christian descent who have been tossed about by the vagaries of historical circumstance and who have largely forgotten our rootage in Moses and in Jesus. And the preacher's task, I submit, is to *re-text* this community: to turn the imagination and the practice of the community back to its most elemental assurances and claims. The preacher gives up trying to replicate the work of thirteenth-century Moses or tenth-century Nathan or eighth-century Elijah or fifth-century Daniel, and takes on the work of a second-century *scribe*. Scribes, after all, do not try to *be* Moses before Pharaoh. Their job is to keep that confrontation between truth and power alive and available to the community through acts of textual interpretation and imagination. Scribes also remind the community that Moses, Nathan, Elijah, and Daniel do *not*, in fact, have the starring roles in their texts; YHWH does. YHWH—the one who promises and delivers and commands—is the key character. YHWH—the one who endlessly summons people away from a life without promise and deliverance and commands, and into a world that the text provides and proposes as normative—is the star. And this key character is not enacted by the preacher, but acts in and for God's own self through the scribe's re-performance of the text.

The task of re-texting requires two things of the Preacher-Scribe. First, it asks us *to be a text-man or a text-woman:* to study it, to trust it, to engage it, to be led by it, to submit our modernist assumptions to it, and to have confidence that *this text*—despite all its vagaries and violence, its unbearable harshness and confounding cadences—is the one that merits our primal attention as a word of life. Second, the task of re-texting requires us *to attend to the listening congregation in a particular way.* In part, they already know this text. Yet some in the congregation are *textless,* believing that they can live out of their autonomous experience without any text,[2] while others bring a *weak, thin text* of technological, therapeutic military consumerism that is an odd mix of moralism, market ideology, self-congratulations, and anxiety. The scribe, then, does not do text-work in a vacuum, but (a) in the face of resistance that rejects any text, or (b) in the face of thin text that claims excessive and disproportionate authority, or (c) in the presence of those who are inclined to this text but who have little clue about how to hear it so that it can function as identity-giving.

IV

Let us return, now, to the four texts we considered earlier, imagining how the Preacher-Scribe might go about the task of re-texting in these proclamatory encounters. To reiterate, the task of re-texting, or scribal refraction, is to let the text itself be the resource for offering an alternative imagination, energy, and identity for the community. In these texts, we will see that truth-speaking-to-power is very much present, but that the notions of truth and power are playfully open. We will also carefully distinguish between what is *in the text* and *our engagement with the text.*

1. *Moses addressing Pharaoh.* The transaction of the text is simple: YHWH commands; Moses confronts; Pharaoh resists; YHWH prevails. The narrative process maps the world in terms of the tension between power and powerlessness. Included in that map are the social world (power grids in families and churches and seminaries, for example) and the economic world (tension between labor and capital, between haves and have-nots). The text, then, may invite us to play many roles, or even all of them, in the drama. We may listen as the one addressed or as the one sent. We may imagine ourselves in Pharaoh's role, as one resistant to address, *or* we may imagine another take on Pharaoh's role—playing it, perhaps, as one willing to be addressed and to repent, so that what follows is a different outcome to the Exodus narrative. But note well: scribal refraction is not excessively hot about *relevance.* While the text, in our scribal imagination, may send out lines of connection and allude to our own contexts, *for the most part the interpretation stays within the text and lets the listening congregation stay within the text—without being scolded or shamed or threatened.*

2. *Nathan addressing David.* The situation here is somewhat different. Nathan is the literary figure who brings to speech both the guilt and the favor that surely hovered over David. Unlike Pharaoh, David is a child of the Torah. He knows about the ten commandments. But until the matter with Bathsheba and Uriah is uttered as a

prophetic speech of judgment, David does not need to deal with the problem, and perhaps *cannot* deal with it. Thus Nathan is the voicing of the relentless, unvoiced agony of a failed child of Torah. He doesn't say anything *new* to David; he says what was already known but waiting to be voiced again—and indeed, that is why David caught the parable and confessed so quickly. Nathan seems like a harsh judge, but in fact, his work is to *relieve* David, to *unburden* him (albeit in costly ways), so that even in David's thin, failed life, he may try again to become who he is. The speech of judgment, then, makes available to David the givenness of Torah from which David had momentarily imagined himself immune. The Preacher-Scribe invites the congregation to ponder the deep voicing of failure, the givenness of Torah, the costly way of forgiveness, and the wonder of beginning again in a post-forgiveness life.

3. *Elijah addressing Ahab.* The third case is severe and without pastoral nuance. We have seen that Pharaoh is an *outsider* to the Israelite tradition who does not know, while David is an *insider* to the Israelite traditions who knows. Ahab, in contrast to both, is an ambiguous figure: he is *an insider who should have known*. The fact that he does not press the dispute with Naboth in the first place indicates that at least on some level, he must have known. But Ahab has lived a long time outside the tradition. He has rooted his life in the outsider Jezebel, who does not know or care a thing about Israelite covenantalism. Perhaps Ahab admired her freedom and ruthlessness. Perhaps he yearned to be as free from ambiguity as was she. Perhaps he feared her and wished he had the courage to resist her. Or perhaps Ahab is simply double-minded, unwilling and unable to choose between a Torah tradition he is supposed to know and an acquisitive alternative that suits him better; maybe that is why he pouts, turns his head to the wall, and won't eat. *He could not decide.*

I think on any given day that we do this text, Ahab will not be the only one in the room who does not want to decide. He will not be the only one whose energy is sapped by ambivalence. The resistant Jezebel, who *has* decided (and who then takes ten long, slow chapters to die the inescapable death God ordains for the resistant), will not be the only one who is waiting for God's slow-but-sure, post-decision judgment; nor will the properly repentant but still-depressed Ahab be the only one who eventually does the right thing, but still can't get over his dejection at having given up Jezebel's appealing, self-indulgent alternative. The congregation can and will participate in all these parts because they know Naboth's "vineyard": it is whatever we want but are not entitled to. Indeed, the phrase "Naboth's Vineyard" is a study of a review of U.S. policy in Central America written by the Associate Secretary of State, Sumner Wells, under the administration of Franklin Roosevelt; Wells cast the United States as Ahab in relation to Naboth's vineyard in Central America. We live in a world and a system of endless strategies for taking the vineyard of the little guy, not unlike the one lamb belonging to the poor man. Naboth, Nathan . . . our narrative imagination is peopled by phalanxes of old characters who keep turning up to expose our entitlements that are, in fact, *seizures,* rapacious seizures, that have the smell of death about them. The congregation will hear. They will know.

4. *Daniel addressing Nebuchadnezzar.* The fourth case is something of a fairy tale, but it is engaging nonetheless, because it suggests that *unlimited power*—that is, uncurbed entitlement, and the absolutizing of one's personal claims—leads not only to loss, but to *insanity.* The narrative poses the question of how our practice of power in the world may be a practice of madness, and indeed a cause of craziness. Yet still the narrative holds out promise. Unlike the accounts of Pharaoh and Ahab (less so with David), there is here a chance of rehabilitation and restoration to power. The move from self-destructive insanity to restoration and sanity is marked by two moves: *the act of doxology* (publicly ceding authority beyond oneself to God Most High, and surrendering oneself to the one praised), which then triggers *the notion of obedience* (imitating YHWH, the God of mercy and righteousness, in the practice of Torah obedience).

Scribes are modest people. They do not claim too much for themselves. They do not push people into corners, nor do they issue strong imperatives. They tell the truth and stage text-time for engagement with that truth.

- They invite people who live without texts to try a text that has holy presence at its center, presence that shapes the world toward life.
- They invite people with thin texts to a thickness that cannot be had apart from the God who governs.

- They invite people already in this text to ponder more closely, to notice nuance and cadence and lines sent out to contemporary life.

The text is a voice of truth, albeit an elusive one. Yet when text-time is well managed, truth *does* speak to power—*but not through the advocacy of the preacher*. The Preacher-Scribe functions more like a pastoral therapist, who seeks to let power of illusion and repression be addressed by old, deep texts that swirl around us. Like a therapist, the Preacher-Scribe does not own the text; the text lives in, with, and under the memory of the community. So the Preacher-Scribe gets out of the center and out of the way. The Preacher-Scribe *trusts the text* to have a say through the power of the Spirit rather than the power of the preacher; *trusts the listening congregation* to make the connections it is able to make; and *trusts the deep places of truthful power and powerful truth* that draw us in and send us forth in repentance, a turn that makes all things new.

V

I finish with two concluding comments.

Jesus taught his disciples about the kingdom of God by means of parables, not by confrontation. In Matthew 13:40-50, he says to them, "Have you understood all of this?" (Jesus is clearly a teacher and is asking for feedback!) The disciples answer, "Yes." And Jesus says to them, *"Therefore, every scribe who has been trained for the kingdom of heaven is like the master of a household who brings out of his treasure what is new and what is old."* And, the text says, when Jesus had finished these parables, he left that place.

It cannot be unimportant that Jesus instructs his disciples by reference to scribes. Perhaps he invites them to be scribes trained for the new age; perhaps he references himself as a scribe. Either way, the scribe here is nothing like the stereotypical Pharisee or hypocrite, but instead is an agent who is equipped for God's coming new reign. And that agent, for the sake of God's newness, is to have *a rich treasure*—things old and things new. Think for a moment about the scribal preoccupation with *text*. What could a treasure be for a scribe, if it is not *a treasure of texts*—old texts, new interpretations—all for the purpose of opening us to God's newness? This teaching of Jesus may be an invitation to re-imagine the preaching role as the management of old things and new things for the sake of God's rule. And of course, that is what the scribes did:

- The old text of Moses and Pharaoh for the new Exodus community,
- The old text of Nathan and David for the new monarchy,
- The old text of Elijah and Ahab for the sake of Israel's future,
- The old text of Daniel and Nebuchadnezzar for the sake of the new world of Jews and Gentiles.

Old and new . . . coming rule . . . and the scribes manage.

William Cavanaugh, in his remarkable book *Torture and Eucharist*, tells how, albeit belatedly, the Roman Catholic Church in Chile came to understand that the community-creating of Eucharist was a powerful antidote to the community-destroying torture of the dictator Augusto Pinochet. They discovered that Eucharist was stronger than torture. At the end of his book, Cavanaugh writes about a fictional character, Carlos, in a novel concerning this crisis. He refers to "Carlos" but, in fact, means the community-creating capacity of the church.

> Carlos's gift is more than just the gift of seeing; his stories about people can actually alter reality. . . . Carlos's friends nevertheless remain skeptical, convinced that Carlos cannot confront tanks with stories, helicopters with mere imagination. . . . Carlos . . . rightly grasps that the contest is not between imagination and the real, but between two types of imagination, that of the generals and that of their opponents.[3]

Carlos, in the novel, comments,

> We have to believe in the power of imagination because it is all we have, and ours is stronger than theirs.[4]

And Cavanaugh himself adds,

> To participate in the Eucharist is to live inside God's imagination. It is to be caught up into what is really real, the body of Christ.[5]

Think about scribes for the kingdom, engaged in an imagination that is stronger than the imagination of military consumerism. This counter-imagination is the treasure of the scribes of the kingdom. It happens by *texts* and bread and *texts* and wine and *texts* and *texts* and *texts*. The oldest stories become the newest songs. Stories from Moses and Nathan and Elijah and Daniel and a host of others' old stories let the church sing—free, dangerous, energized, filled with courage. So much depends on scribes who are trained for the kingdom.

This paper was presented at the Festival of Homiletics in Chicago
at Fourth Presbyterian Church on May 21, 2002.
This is a revised version of an essay I originally published
in the Scottish Journal of Theology.

Notes

1. It may well be that that is all that Nathan said, all that he needed to say, all that he dared to say. Following Martin Noth, the critics have concluded that after the narrative, in its artistic coolness, comes the intensity of the Deuteronomist to pin things down so that nobody misunderstands the truth uttered and the power deconstructed: "Why have you despised the word of the LORD, to do what is evil in his sight? You have struck down Uriah the Hittite with the sword, and have taken his wife to be your wife, and have killed him with the sword of the Ammonites. Now therefore the sword shall never depart from your house, for you have despised me, and have taken the wife of Uriah the Hittite to be your wife. Thus says the LORD: I will raise up trouble against you from within your own house; and I will take your wives before your eyes, and give them to your neighbor, and he shall lie with your wives in the sight of this very sun. For you did it secretly; but I will do this thing before all Israel, and before the sun" (2 Sam 12:9-12).

2. George A. Lindbeck, *The Nature of Doctrine: Religion and Theology in a Postliberal Age* (Philadelphia: Westminster, 1984), 31–32.

3. William T. Cavanaugh, *Torture and Eucharist: Theology, Politics, and the Body of Christ* (Oxford: Blackwell, 1998), 278.

4. Ibid., 279.

5. Ibid.

On Reading the Old Testament

We begin as eager beavers,
    partly in gladness for new tasks,
    partly in anxiety for much work to do,
    partly in fear at all the unlearning we must now face.

We begin yet again another new beginning
        as our learning always does—
    only to discover yet again
    that our beginnings are in the midst of your continuing,
        your continuing sovereign demand,
        your continuing gracious mercy,
        your continuing dread-filled presence.

So we put our beginning down in your continuing,
        confident of the edges of our faith,
        and so free for the big things now to be
    learned and received and enacted.

As a class in Old Testament we pray as the leisure class
        with much free, unencumbered time entrusted to us,
        we imagine ourselves to be highly burdened,
            but in fact we are deeply privileged.

We pray this day that we have received from you,
    that we may live it back to you
        in wonder, love, and praise. Amen.

September 6, 2002

Waiting in Central Casting

Luke 12:13-34; Colossians 3:1-6

This is a drama about greed. It has four characters in it. As we go along, you can decide which role you would like to play. If you get really engaged in the story, you have my permission to play more than one role. I will simply take care that you identify the roles carefully, so you know what you are doing.

I

The first role is a character named "someone"; he comes with his brother whom we may identify as "someone's brother." This is a small role, and you can get this part over with quickly. It is nonetheless an important role, because everything in the story depends upon it:

"Someone in the crowd said to Jesus."

It is an anonymous voice in the crowd, not one of his disciples. It is a voice in the world, not of the church. He said, "Tell my brother to divide the family inheritance with me." That's what you get if you have a brother. The brother is likely the older brother who was named the executor; he is shifty and cunning, so that the first brother thinks he is not being treated fairly. And likely he is not. Maybe the speaking brother was desperate for some inherited money. The text may suggest that he already had a lot, but he wants more. He will never have enough, and it sets him against his brother. He wants what his brother has, his or not, and this is a kind of scolding, grasping anxiety in his voice, suggesting that it is never enough. If you want to play this role, you have to practice a tone of grasping, scolding anxiety.

II

The second role is a rich man. He has a name, but we will come to that later. I think he is made to look, in the parable, a lot like the brother

21

in the crowd. But he is different. He is a prosperous can-do guy who is always thinking and planning and buying and selling and trading and getting. He talks a lot. But he lives alone. He inhabits a world that has no other residents. He is a lonely rich man. Perhaps he is lonely because he has so much land that he is a far piece from the nearest neighbor. He talks a lot, but he is required to talk only to himself, as his abundance has eliminated anyone else from his conversation.

> We see him in two postures. First, we see him *planning:*
> What shall I do? I have got no more storage place.

Pause. Answer:

> I will tear down the old barn, because it is so small. In its place I will build a bigger barn to hold more. God, I can't believe I have so much and more coming. Thank you, Jesus!

And after he plans, he pauses to *celebrate*. He holds a party. Probably drinks and music and dancing, but nobody comes. Small party. Now, finally, he speaks his own name:

> "Soul, psyche, self, anonymous, unconnected, isolated guy with abundance."

So the drinking started and the eating and the making merry. All by himself. You can imagine, he is safe, perhaps drunk by now, alone, content, alone, vulnerable, alone, safe, alone, rich, alone, asleep, alone. It is not a happy role to play. But some play it anyway in their muchness.

III

There is a third role, brief but decisive. It is God. Would you like to play God? You can, but I do not think anyone should have that role all to one's self. So I suggest we share this role and all of us think about playing it. It is a rather heavy role for a party-crasher. "But God said!" How did God get in here to the party? The man was all alone, but God violates the solitude, enters the party, and addresses the guy, the one whose name is *self*.

God calls the man by a different name, not self. He calls him by his right name. God is the one who knows the names of all the players. Your name is not self; your name is *fool*. You act your name, fool that you are, so greedy that you have isolated yourself, so acquisitive that you have lost your soul, your self. You have been so covetous that you have organized your life against your own personhood. We can all play this role with this one word. Say it with me: *"FOOL!"*

Being God is demanding, because you must sometimes speak the unwelcome truth when everyone else is engaged in deception. The truth is, you are going to die. You not only have to tell the truth, you have to have an eloquent phrase for your verdict. You are going to die, because you are not "rich toward God." You are rich for yourself, but rich for yourself is misdirected wealth that kills, because your true character is to turn your wealth back to God and God's will for the world. God quotes the book of Proverbs: Foolishness brings death; you cannot spend enough money or own enough land to break the connection between foolishness and death. That is the verdict of the story.

IV

If you are lucky, you will be in the fourth role, the disciples. The disciples are the ones who have watched this drama from behind the one-way mirror in the classroom. And now the teacher comes to ask the observers: "What do you think this is about?"

> He said, "Do not be anxious; do not be a fool; do not choose death."
> He said, "Your father will get you what you need without your greediness."
> He said, "Get to work for the kingdom, and the rest will take care of itself."
> He said, "Do not be afraid and if not afraid, not greedy, not coveting, not acquisitive."
> He said, "Live lean and rejoice."

The disciples are lucky because they are invited to an alternative. The disciples are the ones invited and empowered by Jesus for a different way in the world, outside the aggression, outside the fear, outside the death trap, invited to be rich toward God, having put the treasure where it belongs, not called fool, called "little flock," little beloved flock, invited differently, not to death. The party to which the disciples are invited is not one of isolation and death. There are at this party lots of folk, lots of joy, lots of food, lots of friends, and no voice of death.

<h1 style="text-align:center">V</h1>

Perhaps you noticed I did not mention Jesus yet. Well, he is the director of central casting. He decides who belongs appropriately in what role. So consider the options, because the assignment of parts will be made soon:

- The someone with a brother, with grasping, scolding anxiety;
- The rich man, all alone at his party, with a death sentence for greed;
- God, who calls things by their right names and breaks the deception;
- The disciples, the ones authorized to do differently.

Central casting will act soon. You may want to practice for your preferred role, because nobody is assigned a role that is unsuitable.

I know this sermon is supposed to be about economics and the global rat race. But the text seemed to me so much more interesting than that. The text is being played out just below the surface of our daily lives. It is a sub-version of reality. If you get in it, you will find conventional economics subverted. Oh, here comes central casting with the assignments. Are you ready?

Presented to the Wisconsin Council of Churches / October 3, 1998

On Reading Psalm 1

You voice the worlds into being,
You voice the church into obedience,
You voice us, now and then, into newness,
You speak and call into existence that which does not exist.

You speak and address us,
        and make all things new.

And we should answer you:
        we in our shabbiness before your splendor,
        we in our timidity before your magnificence,
        we in our poverty before your wealth,
        we in our foolishness before your wisdom.

We stammer and stutter and pause and parry,
        silent, mute, reluctant,
        with only one gift back to you—that of tongue.

So for our tongues—thousands and thousands of them,
        we give you thanks:
that we may speak back to you your wonder,
that we may sing back to you your presence,
that we may vow back to you our obedience.
        You speak and we are,
        You listen and we are voiced,
            always again on our way rejoicing. Amen.

June 17, 2002 (Montreat)

On Signal: Breaking the Vicious Cycles

Leviticus 25:8-24; Isaiah 61:1-4; Luke 4:16-30

My father-in-law, Patrick D. Miller, was a distinguished Presby-terian minister—pastor at Druid Hills Church, denomina-tional executive, and moderator of the General Assembly. One day he and I were discussing how to translate the Lord's Prayer . . . "for-give us our trespasses, forgive us our sins, forgive us our debts." He said, only half joking, "I would rather have my debts forgiven than my sins." Of course, he was a Calvinist, and Calvinists are the ones who think most about money and loans and debts, and interest, and taxes, and capital gains, and wealth. In such a world, forgiveness of debts matters a lot.

Long before my father-in-law, Moses—probably a secret Calvin-ist—announced to Israel God's will for money and property, one of the most distinctive marks of biblical ethics. It is called Jubilee. Moses—the secret Calvinist—declared as God's will: every fifty years you must give back to the people the land and property that is inalien-ably theirs that they have lost in the rough and tumble of the economy. You must give it back, even if you own it legally and it is properly yours. You must give it back, because in the end it is theirs and not yours, inalienably. The start of the occasion for the return of property is signaled by a trumpet, in Hebrew *yabal,* from which we get Jubilee, Jubilation, a huge celebration of bringing things back to where they ought to be. So imagine, when the *yabal* sounds, when the signal is given, everybody returns property, everybody cancels debts, every-body breaks off the mad scramble of accumulation and acquisition. It is a signal not unlike the great gavel that ends the fury of Wall Street every day, only it signifies something very different. At the center of biblical faith is a command from God that curbs economic transac-tions by an act of communal sanity that restores everyone to proper place in the economy, because life in the community of faith does not consist in getting more but in sharing well. We focus on Jubilee because this is Trinity's fiftieth year (Trinity Presbyterian Church, Atlanta, Georgia), and the *yabal* is sounding in Trinity; when we hear it we think "Jubilee." I want to tell you three things about Jubilee as you ponder how Trinity should practice it at the end of fifty glorious years.

I

Jubilee is a *concrete, material, economic act* that is undertaken with discipline and intentionality. It is not just a kind thought or a good intention or a religious idea. It is about money and property being transferred. That preoccupation with money and property is central to biblical faith. One could think that the Bible is all about sex. In truth, the Bible is much more concerned with money and property than it is about sexuality. And at the center of its economic teaching is this business of Jubilee.

While those old folk did not know about the intricacies of the modern market and moving wealth by electronic means, they knew all about commerce. Indeed, it is likely that the word "Canaanite," the ones feared the most by Israel, means "traders" who bought and sold and moved money and goods. When Moses wanted to state the distinctive mark of Israel alongside the Canaanites, he knew that the distinction is not territorial or ethnic or linguistic. It is ethical. Moses observed the working of the market, the practice of accumulation and acquisitiveness and greed and monopoly. He observed, as anyone can see, that in the long run the operations of accumulation and acquisitiveness tend to monopoly, so that some end up with a lot and some end up with a little or with none, have and have-nots, wealth and poverty. And what Moses figured out is that such a process is an impossible way to run a community. And so he announces in that long speech in Leviticus 25, at the end of forty-nine years of accumulation, the property will be returned to its proper owners (vv. 27-28). The land cannot be sold to perpetuity (v. 23), that is, irreversibly, because the land belongs to God and not to the accumulators. God wants the little ones, who always lose in the market game, to have their stuff. When the signal is given, the vicious cycles of accumulation are broken, wealth is divested back to the ones who do not have it. It is an act of divestment.

This practice of *divestment on signal* is *exceedingly difficult,* and folks do not want to do it. It is the most difficult, most demanding, most outrageous requirement of biblical faith. It surely seems so in the modern world with our deep practices of accumulation and our intense yearning to have ours and keep ours and make it grow. Indeed, in all my teaching of the Bible, when this subject comes, somebody—seminarian, pastor, lay person inevitably asks and wants to be reassured, "There is no evidence that they really did this, is there?" But it is not really a question. It is an act of resistance. Because we do not want to divest for the sake of someone else. I do not want to return to someone else what I have been able to acquire. What is mine is not his! It is likely here, more than anywhere, that the Bible questions our usual assumptions about our life in the world.

The command, however, is no more objectionable now than it was then. In a related law, Moses chides Israel:

> Be careful that you do not entertain a mean thought,
> thinking, the year of release is near and therefore view
> your needy neighbor with hostility and give nothing . . .
> do not consider it a hardship. (Deut 15:9, 18)

But the most dramatic resistance to Jubilee is reported in Luke 4. Jesus came to the synagogue and read the scripture lesson from Isaiah 61:

> He has sent me to proclaim release to the captives . . . to let
> the oppressed go free, to proclaim the year of the Lord's
> favor.

What this text is doing is proclaiming Jubilee, "the year of the Lord's favor." To let the oppressed go free is to cancel debts, to let the poor back into the economy with their rightful stuff. And then he made it worse; he said, "Today this scripture has been fulfilled in your hearing." What he meant was, "I am the Jubilee. Isaiah wrote about it. I am going to enact it." And he set about giving social power and social access and social goods to the poor and excluded. And says Luke, "They were filled with rage." They tried to kill him by throwing him off a cliff, and he barely escaped. They did not want to hear about the Jubilee that would curb their accumulation, not even for Jesus. It is a hard command.

The only reason one might obey such a hard command that is concrete, material, and economic divestment is that we have a *different, large vision of the future.* We know what is promised and what will be, by the power of God. The command is to serve the great social vision of the Gospel, because that vision of God will only become reality when there is enough human obedience. This vision of God is not a vision of accumulation and monopoly so that those who have the most when they die win. This vision of God's future is not about angels who have gone to heaven floating around in the sky with their loved ones. This vision, rather, is about God's kingdom coming on earth as it already is in heaven. God's rule where the practices of justice and mercy and kindness and peaceableness are every day the order of the day. It is a vision of the world as a peaceable neighborliness in which no one is under threat, no one is at risk, no one is in danger, because all are safe, all are valued, all are honored, all are cared for. And this community of peaceableness will come only when the vicious cycles of violent accumulation are broken.

You see, what Moses understood, that we all understand in our society, is that you cannot have a viable, peaceable, safe urban community when deep poverty must live alongside huge wealth, when high privilege is visible alongside endless disadvantage in health and housing and education. You can have some inequities, but the inequities must be curbed by a practice of neighborliness that knows every day that rich and poor, haves and have-nots, are in it together and must find ways of being together as neighbors in common.

From the outset of the Bible, certainly in God's command of Sinai and surely in the ministry of Jesus, *signals of neighborliness are endlessly enacted.* That finally is what is odd and true and demanding and glorious about the Gospel, that God wills and acts toward a neighborliness that curbs greed, vetoes fear, and removes the causes of violence. We baptized people are the ones who have signed on for this vision and act toward it. The poem Jesus quotes from Isaiah 61 ends with a marvelous anticipation:

> a garland instead of ashes,
> gladness instead of sadness,
> praise instead of feebleness,

they shall build up the ancient ruins,
they shall repair the ruined city,
the devastation of many generations. (Isa 61:3-4)

When the cycles are broken by divestment, newness comes on a large scale.

IV

And now comes Trinity—fifty years—Jubilee to face this hard prac-tice of a glorious vision. There is no single recipe for how to enact Jubilee. But let me observe three zones in which *divestment will make newness possible:*

Every family I know lives partly by an intricate practice of debt management, of old wounds remembered, of old properties held, old angers, old resentments. In Montreat we have an old pie safe that has been there at least thirty-five years, to my knowledge. Periodically but not often, a cousin observes, "that really belongs to me." Jubilee is a chance in our families to break old cycles of resentment and hurt, so that when the signal is given, debts are forgiven, sins are par-doned, and newness may come close to home, beyond our best expectations.

At Trinity Church, what a chance now as the signal sounds. Trin-ity occupies a peculiar position in Atlanta and in Presbyterianism. Your size, your wealth, your special vision, your deep compassion, your generous spirit are known among us all. Trinity may now think of deep and bold gestures of Jubilee, costly enough and significant enough to impact the truth of the city, not something safe and modest and in-house, but something that gives back to the city enough that will make neighborliness possible in fresh, perhaps dramatic ways. It is the business of such a church to do that.

Such a powerful assemblage as Trinity, soon or late, may think about Jubilee as *obedience concerning public policy issues.* The ques-tion as public policy has nothing that I can think of to do with being Republican or Democrat, conservative or liberal, even capitalist or socialist. It has to do with our deep gospel conviction that our society is increasingly becoming a jungle of fear and danger, and will keep on that way . . . unless and until we think seriously about neighborliness between haves and have-nots, about taxation and all the pieces of Jubilee economy.

On this fifty years of Trinity, listen for the signal, the *yabal*, the trumpet. It is a *summons to divest*, to *let in an evangelical future*. Jesus is our signal. The jubilee is done, so that,

> the blind see, the lame walk, lepers are cleansed, the
> dead are raised, and the poor have their debts canceled.
> (Luke 7:22)

My father-in-law had it right. The best thing is to have our debts forgiven. That is why we pray,

> Forgive us our debts . . .
> as we forgive our debtors.

Trinity Presbyterian Church, Atlanta, Georgia / November 15, 1998
on the occasion of Fiftieth Anniversary

On Reading Psalm 116

The pattern of faith and life is clear enough among us.
>   You give and we receive,
>   You give and overwhelm us and we receive,
>   You give far more abundantly than we can ask,
>> or imagine . . .
>> and we receive.

>   You give life and breath to the world and we receive.
>   You give miracles of deliverance and newness,
>> and we receive.
>   You give rain and sunshine and food,
>> and we receive.
>   You give yourself in this strange Jesus,
>> and we receive.
>   You take and bless and break and give,
>> and we receive . . .
>>> nourished, quenched.

>   You give and sometimes we are among the tenth
>>   that thanks:
>>> thanks with our words;
>>> thanks with our study;
>>> thanks with our money;
>>> thanks with our lives;
>>   our abiding thanks, gratitude transient when contrasted
>>> with your abiding gifts. Amen.

October 3, 2002

Strategies for Humanness

Psalm 32; Matthew 4:1-11 / First Sunday in Lent

This is a very old-fashioned Gospel text about Jesus being tempted by the devil and resisting. It suits the beginning of Lent well. But the Gospel of Matthew is a *church book*. It cares about what the church is and how to be the church. So what if this Gospel reading is not about "the temptation of Jesus," as we say, the last temptation or the first temptation, but it is about the temptation of the church that prays, "Lead us not into temptation"? And what if it is not the devil at work here, but all of those many voices of threat and seduction that seek to talk us out of being the church? Or make it broader. What if it is about all those voices that seek to talk us out of our God-given humanness? I do not need to tell you, do I, that the forces that want to negate our God-given humanness are all around, daily, public, personal, powerful, attentive, and attractive . . . forces that thin us and shorten us and slot us until we are diminished. Jesus is offered here as a guide and model and resource for how to resist the temptation, how to fend off those voices, how to enact deliberate strategies to be who we are called by God to be.

I

This story of Jesus as guide, model, and resource for a different humanity has a brief introduction. It situates Jesus this way: He fasted forty days and forty nights. He was under a rigorous discipline of resistance. This statement intends to echo the Moses narrative at Mount Sinai when Moses went away forty days and forty nights. But move then from Jesus to the church and our intention to embrace our God-given humanity.

The beginning place, to which the story always returns us, is the wilderness for fasting. It is the place Elijah went to gather his energies for his vocation, where John the Baptist began, where Paul went to gather for his work. It is disciplined withdrawal and regular retreat, in order to break the familiar linkages and dependencies and loyalties. No more ease in self-indulgence. No more junk food. It might be food that tempts, but maybe not, whatever it is that soaks off our resolve and our intention. The tempter, the temptation, is to grow fat and compliant and complacent and narcoticized, with no edge for the issues of our God-given humanity. But the story of Jesus begins otherwise, with no yielding to such indulgence.

II

As soon as he was hungry from fasting, when he was vulnerable, the voices began their work. The voices always come at us when we are vulnerable and exposed, thinking maybe this time we will give in. The voice wants to seduce Jesus (and us) away from our God-given humanity:

- He was hungry and the voice said, "Make some bread for yourself."
- He was God's man, relying completely on God, and the voice said: "Push the envelope, see how far you can move God beyond common sense, find out if God is real, real enough to support your miracles."
- He was sent on a mission to usher in the new rule of God, to displace all the old ordering of life, and the voice said, "Engage in a little idolatry, and you can have everything you want on your own terms, just give in, just a little."

The voice always comes at Jesus and the church in our moments of yearning vulnerability:

hungry? . . . make bread;
trusting? . . . find out how far;
responsible? . . . get it all by cheating a little.

The voices come when we are *hungry,* when we are *trusting,* when we are *responsible.* When we want to do best and make it right and succeed and finish ahead. The voices come and endanger us. I cannot settle for any of you the question of the form that the voices take, except to say that, without any old-fashioned devil, the voices are everywhere, cunning and dangerous to our health.

But what interests us are not the voices of seduction and temptation and invitation that want us to cheat on our God-given identity.

36

We all know about that in a thousand ways. What interests us is the capacity of Jesus—and perhaps the capacity of the church and perhaps our capacity—to resist such voices. We live in a "give in" culture, give in and go along, join the massage and don't make anything too difficult, and little by little our God-given humanity slips through our fingers. (And only our children notice.)

But Jesus, child of the Torah, was not resourceless. He has his strategies at hand, almost as if he had rehearsed them and was ready when the voices started. He was, perhaps, a Calvinist, because he has a high view of scripture. He understands that to hold for our God-given humanity, you cannot make it up on the spot, but you must be ready with a *thick, palpable response* that silences the voices and defeats the challenge.

He is hungry from fasting and is offered magic bread. But he says, "Man does not live by bread alone." He says, there is more to me than bread, more than money, more than profit, more than commodity, more than exchange value. In this familiar one-liner—man does not live by bread alone—Jesus recalls the entire long sermon from Deuteronomy 8 in which Moses warns Israel about the temptations of being settled and well off. When you get settled, says Moses, and you are rich and you get complacent and self-sufficient and self-congratulatory, remember an earlier time, remember those dangerous times when you and your family did not have enough and did not know from where the next meal was coming, close to starving, as hungry as you are when you fast . . . and remember that God gave you food, just enough. What you learned to do was to live by God's promises of sustenance and well-being that you could not touch or store up. The voice knows that affluence seduces to amnesia, and Jesus has a text of memory ready that he carries with him.

The voice invites Jesus to check out if God can be trusted by jumping off a cliff, and seeing whether God will catch him, testing God by putting Jesus in a situation of jeopardy and forcing God to act. But Jesus says, "Do not test God." Don't use your faith to find out the limits of God's reliability. In that statement, Jesus refutes the voice by a quote from another sermon in Deuteronomy. The context in Deuteronomy is again when Israel is fat and sassy and guaranteed. And Moses says, "Obey what you know; don't test what you do not know . . . obey the core commands of God that are readily at hand . . . love God and love neighbor." That is enough in any crisis.

Moses is in Deuteronomy in the quote used by Jesus. But in Deuteronomy Moses is quoting himself an older story in the book of Exodus. Israel is in the wilderness after the departure from Egypt. Just like Jesus, they are in the wilderness. They want water because they are thirsty, because it is dry in the wilderness. They complain and accuse, and finally Moses hits a rock and water comes gushing out, and they drink. But Moses said, "Do not push God to special miracles." Of course God can do this, but it is not your business to make God into a performer. Your part is not managing miracles. Your part is obedience and that is enough. That is what Jesus says to the voice. No special miracles, just obedience.

The voice said, cheat a little, split your loyalty, worship me a little on the side and I will give you everything. And perhaps he would have. But Jesus has got Moses from Sinai ringing in his ears: "Worship only the LORD your God and serve him alone." No compromise, no half-way faith, no divided loyalty, because divided loyalty will give you everything you want, except your true God-given self, and that comes with an undivided loyalty to the giver of your life.

This story is a meditation on the practice of *faithful living* in contexts that want to seduce. I think that as this story comes up in the lectionary, it is profoundly pertinent to our time and place with God. Everybody knows, liberal and conservative, that ours is a time of cheapening and thinning and forgetting and accommodating, until our power to be freely and faithfully human is too difficult and too demanding. The church is the place where we reflect on and decide to be differently human.

Observe:

We, like Jesus, are addressed by voices that mean us no good;

We, like Jesus, are out in the wilderness of confusion with few resources.

We, like Jesus, are put there seemingly empty-handed but in fact not empty-handed. He had the book of Deuteronomy with him. He had his Bible with him. He had the whole, deep resource of faith memories that are old and trusted and reliable. He was not out there alone, but in the company of many ancient, faithful, trusted voices that told him who he was.

He was not finally at risk, because he was supplied with resources that made the challenge of evil easy to dispose of. Well, not easy, but easy because he was nurtured for a thousand years in proper, adequate, bold responses.

The text is faithful to the end of the encounter. The text reports, "The devil left him . . .": The voices of compromise and seduction give up. I am sure the devil said, "Let's find an easier subject. This one takes too much time, because he has too many resources, and we will never defeat him." Jesus will never be robbed of his identity and his vocation. And neither will the folk who travel with him with his resources. Jesus' future, after the devil departed, is this: He immediately calls James and John and Peter and Andrew, right in this same chapter, to build the new humanity of those who know who they are, who are deep for obedience, and who are prepared to be with Jesus in his work.

III

There is a final note to this story, a conclusion when the devil gave up and quit and left. Immediately, the story says, "Suddenly angels came and ministered to him." Right away, abruptly, just as soon as he resisted—but not before—food came. He is still hungry, still fasting. He refused the food of death that would have robbed him of his identity. And now comes the bread of life, because this good God gives miraculously to the obedient. There is no cheap food. It is given to those who hang in with ancient memories that withstand the pressures of thinning. These same strategies for humanness are of course still on offer. They are given and guaranteed, however, only for the Torah people who obey, only to those who try wilderness away from junk food. The news is that the angels will come promptly when the devil has been resisted and has failed. Maybe it is the devil, among others, whom Paul refers to in Romans:

> I am sure that neither powers nor heights of ecstasy nor
> depths of despair can separate us from God.

Jesus is not separated from God in this narrative. He is well connected to God. As are we, the people of Jesus.

Second Presbyterian Church, Indianapolis, Indiana / February 21, 1999

On Reading Psalm 104

Yours is the sky with its water,
Yours is the land with its plants,
Yours is the deep earth with mineral resources,
Yours . . . and we arrive each day
               like gaping little birds . . .
         with hungers we cannot satisfy,
         with thirst we cannot quench,
         with deep inhaling of the gift of your breath,
         with safety we cannot generate,
         with rest we can only receive.

You give and give and give . . .
         a gift that keeps giving
And we? We receive
               grace upon grace,
               bread endlessly,
               water without which we die,
         We receive
Occasionally imagining we possess.

But mainly we receive and discover that
         the dialect of your conversation
               is all about gift and grace and gratitude.

We take a deep breath—of your breath—
         and yearn to speak your idiom,
               because the rest is gibberish. Amen.

September 17, 2002

On People Who Do "Great Things"

2 Kings 8:1-6; Matthew 10:5-26

There are two things you need to know about Elisha, this dynamo of social turmoil in ancient Israel. First, at the beginning, he asked his mentor, Elijah, for "a double share of your spirit" (2 Kgs 2:9). We are not told so, but apparently he received a double share. He became a man with courage, energy, and power who wades into the impossible and makes things new. Second, his ministry, as we know it, is a lifelong capacity to open up the world to God's power and thereby to transform social relationships. He is a human agent who embodies and enacts the newness of God in the world. And so we are given a narrative collection of the stories that remember his astonishing deeds that are nothing short of miraculous. I will not linger over these stories or go into detail, but will move along to our text.

I

The narrative in 2 Kings 8:1-6 is different from the miracle stories that come earlier. Here the narrative reflects those earlier accomplishments of the prophet. As this text opens, Elisha is yet again with a woman in an emergency. We are told that she is the woman "whose son he had restored to life" back in chapter 4. She is the woman from Shunem who had received an Easter wonder from Elisha. He raised her dead son to life. But now she is in a different crisis, one about which she does not yet know. Elisha tells her about a coming famine. A famine may be caused by careless human activity, such as war and siege. It may also be reckoned as a curse from God. Either way, says the prophet, it will last seven long years. And she must leave town or she will starve to death. He does not tell her where to go, only that she must go where there is food.

She obeys his directive. Ordinarily one would go to Egypt, the breadbasket. But she does not get that far. She stops with the

Philistines, of all people. There is surely irony that this "unclean" people has food while the famine is localized precisely among God's own people, Israel.

She remains with the Philistines for seven years, as he had said. When the famine is over in Israel, she returns home. But her land and her house are gone. Of course! One cannot leave property unattended that long. She has lost it. A vulnerable woman in a patriarchal society would lose everything. Perhaps it has been sold at public auction. Perhaps it fell into the hands of the crown or one of the crown's favorite bankers. She no longer has access or title. And so she files a formal complaint with the king who is to adjudicate such matters. The text says, "outcry." She protests her loss to the highest court of appeal.

Meanwhile . . . the king, son of Ahab, is having a chat with—of all people—Gehazi. Gehazi is Elisha's "minder" who was with him when he had raised the woman's son from the dead. It is a little odd that this aide to the prophet is at ease in the king's office, but perhaps it is his day off. In any case, it seems a casual conversation.

And then the king says to Gehazi, seemingly without warning and out of the blue, "Tell me all the great things Elisha has done." Perhaps:

- the king is proud to have such a miracle worker in his realm and wants the full detail;
- the king is frightened of such a magic man who is more powerful than is he, and he wants surveillance;
- the king is sarcastic, cynical about miracles.

In any case, the king asks, so Gehazi begins to answer the king's query. In Hebrew, Gehazi speaks only four words about the dead son who is brought to life again. He had many miracles of Elisha to report to the king, but he focuses on the most radical of these, the Easter resurrection. This miracle of resurrection goes along with the others that are narrated about healing and feeding and canceling debts. The king asked for "great things." What one needs to know about this exchange is that characteristically only God does "great things." The term is reserved for the great public miracles of God. What is so spectacular about Elisha is that this *human agent* does *divine miracles in the world*. He does many divine miracles as human agent, the most astonishing is this Easter.

Before Gehazi can utter more than four words, however, the woman bursts into the king's office with her outcry. She is tense and eager and unafraid. As she storms in, Gehazi says out of the corner of his mouth to the king, "This is the Easter mother." It is her son who was raised to new life. That makes the great thing flesh and blood to the king, for before him is this real, live mother accompanied by her real, live son, before the very eyes of the king in his own office.

Gehazi says no more about "great things." The king now interviews the woman and makes a remarkable royal decision, remarkable if you remember his father Ahab and Naboth's vineyard:

- give her land back to her;
- give her all the revenue produced by the land in her seven years of absence.

This is the antithesis of "back taxes." This is "back revenue," fully restored to life in the land, restored to life, as was her son. The king has worked an economic Easter. I think he did this "great thing" for the woman concerning real estate, because he had heard about prophetic "great things" and replicated it with a royal "great thing." To be sure, the great thing of a king is not like a great thing of the prophet; it is more mundane, more material, seemingly more routine. But he does it. The story seems to be about the prophet, but the immediate hero is the king. Both prophet and king in turn make things new by enacting "great things," divine miracles by human agents.

II

Now what I want to tell you is this. The New Testament story of Jesus has a peculiar word for human agents who do divine miracles in the world: It is *disciples*, those who have been with Jesus so long that they become like Jesus. So think about,

- the great things done by Elisha, including an Easter,
- the great thing done by the king . . . land reform,
- the great things done by Jesus, new life,
- the great things done by the disciples, among whom you people are surely to be counted.

I identify five marks of these disciples, the human agents who do divine miracles in the real world:

1. The disciples are sent out to *do transformative acts* in the world that other people regard as impossible:

> The kingdom of heaven has come near. Cure the sick, raise
> the dead, cleanse the lepers, cast out demons. (vv. 7-8)

The reason these actions can be done is that the world is under new management, even if the world does not yet recognize that new rule. All of these actions—healing, cleansing, raising the dead, casting out demons (and we might add, land reform)—are in order to right the world and make it congruent with the new management of the kingdom of heaven. The disciples are doing "great things" to act decisively against all the old powers that want the world to stay alienated from the rule of God.

2. The disciples are *not to worry about adequate resources:*

> Give without payment. Take no gold, or silver, or copper
> in your belts, no bag for your journey, or two tunics, or
> sandals, or a staff. (vv. 8-9)

This sounds like an assurance of resources to be given at the last moment like manna from heaven. More likely, it is a strategy for a peasant movement, so that the disciples will be fed by their sympathizers as they move across the land. In any case, they are not to have surplus resources so that they may be secure. The inescapable set-up willed by Jesus is an enduring *mismatch* between the large, impossible task and leanness of resources. It is the leanness that makes the miracles possible. And so the mission has always been, at its best, since John and Peter saying:

> Silver and gold we do not have. In the name of Jesus,
> walk. (Acts 3:6)

Lean resources make for uncommon transformative power.

3. The disciples may expect to *encounter fierce resistance* of an institutional kind and expect to be called before the authorities:

They will hand you over to councils and flog you in their synagogues; and you will be dragged before governors and kings because of me. (vv. 17-18)

The Lord who dispatches the disciples as human agents to do divine miracles in the real world knows that resistance will be ruthless and well organized, and will stop at nothing to halt the newness. The authorities hold a huge stake in what is old and failed, and they have all sorts of institutional legitimacy on their side—laws, courts, synagogues, and churches.

Beyond official resistance, there will simply be community hostility, because the initiatives taken for new social relationships are deeply upsetting:

Brother will betray brother to death, and a father his child, and children will rise against parents and have them put to death; and you will be hated by all because of my name. (vv. 21-22)

Newness comes only by abandoning what is old, and the old in all of us never welcomes the threat to how it has been.

4. The disciples, human agents sent to do divine miracles in the real world, are *unafraid,* because they are accompanied and prayed for:

Do not worry about how you are to speak or what you are to say; for what you are to say will be given to you at that time; for it is not you who speak, but the Spirit of your Father speaking through you. (vv. 19-20)

So our reading ends with Jesus' imperative: "Have no fear of them." Fearful people cannot do great things, for fear and anxiety will subvert the courage needed. There is, moreover, a real ground for fearlessness. The disciples are not alone. They are accompanied by the force and power and will of the creator God. That is, they are fully backed by the resolve of the new management that will keep them safe.

Said yet another way, the accompanying spirit is praying for them, so that the disciples are prayed for by God's own life. God's Holy Spirit intercedes and makes petition that all the resolve of the Father may be mobilized for these risk-takers. What a difference to know one is prayed for by the ultimate, heavenly Petitioner.

In the calculus of Jesus, as the *huge task* is matched to *lean resources,* so the *great threat of resistance* is matched *by the Spirit's own determination* on behalf of the disciples. Of course both of these mismatches require courage and resolve that are summarized in the word "faith." The risky life of the disciples is premised on faith that one has signed on and is allied with God's own way in the world.

5. *The outcome is sure,* even if the strategic steps are unclear and uncertain. Discipleship is in the confident matrix of God's own determination to govern the world:

> The one who endures to the end will be saved. (v. 22)

> You will not have gone through all the towns of Israel before the Son of Man comes. (v. 23)

> Nothing is covered up that will not be uncovered, and nothing secret that will not become known. (v. 26)

What is covered up is of course the evidence that God's way will prevail. It is hidden in all the ugly resistance of greed, in all the destructive power of acquisitiveness, in all the legalized force of violence. It is hidden that God's way is powerful; if we go on what we see, we will never go. But it will be uncovered. It will be visible. It will in due time be evident everywhere that God's way will triumph.

III

So imagine, you and I, we, are among the doers of great things. We are the ones entrusted with Easter power. That Easter power is enacted where the dead are raised. But it is also enacted where land is restored to the poor, made visible wherever the sick are cured and there is real health care, uncovered where lepers are cleansed and all the unwelcome outsiders are made insiders, revealed where all the demons are tamed and defeated, and the power of good is made strong.

> Elisha was one who did great things;
> His king was one who did great things;

Jesus was one who did great things;
His disciples continue to do great things:
    lean resources,
    deep resistance,
    unafraid, unafraid because prayed for,
    unafraid, completely unafraid.

Industrial Areas Foundation in Phoenix, Arizona / January 11, 2000

On Reading Psalms 50, 88, 109

God, Lord, sovereign, judge, king, warrior:
> source of power,
> agent of life,
> giver of justice.

> We bask in your faithfulness,
> we live out of your reliability,
> we count completely on your graciousness.

When we cast one eye away from you
> where our vision is deeply fixed
> to the lived reality of our daily life,

We are astonished at how ragged and unsettled life is,
> at how remote our trust in you
> is from the dailyness,
> at how stirred and beset our life
> is with fear and violence,
> with despair and mistrust.

We yearn for simpler times and easier communion with you.

We flee the complexity to your promised clarity,
> and then discover . . . as we are tutored by these old poems . . .
> that you are God exactly in silence,
> in absence,
> in violence,
> in testy retribution and
> in important demand.

Give us nerve to be your people in the unsettledness.

Let us have true home at the end . . . but in the meantime . . .
    on the way ragged but not jaded
            rejoicing but not stupid. You are God in this case
            as in every case. Amen.

September 26, 2002

Uttered beyond Fear

Isaiah 43:1-5; Mark 6:47-52

The entire drama of our faith and the entire truth of our lives is present in this narrative of the storm that takes only six verses to tell. You know very well the plot and the maneuvers made. I will line it out for you one more time. I will line it out for you one more time, because we have nothing better to talk about, and because, if you are like me, you need to hear it yet again.

I

There was a storm; there always seems to be one in the Bible. The NRSV terms it an "adverse wind." Old Testament people call it "chaos." Barth named it *Das Nichtige*, the crushing, irresistible force of disorder as yet untamed and on the loose in our world. That is the recurring place of the disciples, the place of the church, the place of preaching, the place where we all live.

It turns out that the Bible is much more preoccupied with the threat of chaos than it is with sin and guilt, our middle-class fascinations notwithstanding. We have devised ways of forgiveness, of handling sin and guilt, an assurance of pardon, a hug, an embrace. But the storm is not so easy. The storm produces a more elemental, inchoate anxiety, a sense of deep helplessness because you cannot touch it anywhere or handle it or measure it or hold it. It is bottomless in size and beyond measure in force, call it flood, call it Leviathan, call it chaos; all the new scientific theories of the "goodness of chaos" do not touch the deep fear about which the Bible speaks, where preachers must work, and to which pastors must attend.

II

Second Isaiah, my second text, finds the imagery of Chaos useful in order to say what Babylonian exile was like, a deportation and a disconnect from all that was familiar, into a hostile environment that tried to take away all semblance and signs of hope:

This—this exile . . . is like the days of Noah (Isa 54:10). Exactly like the days of Noah when everything comes loose and nothing is reliable or safe. This—the end of the twentieth century—just like the days of the flood, like the days of Noah, all the old certitudes gone, all old power arrangements failed, all old moral convictions in jeopardy. The loss makes us crazy toward each other; we are all prepared to teach preaching and Old Testament in a church and in a context too preoccupied to pay attention or to listen, and we wonder even ourselves.

Only two other things are said:

1. They strained against the adverse wind. Surely without success. Water always wins. Storms are always too strong; it is in their very character to be too strong for us.

2. He wasn't there. The church was on its own, without him in the adverse wind. He was on the land. He was not far away. He was on the shore, out for a walk, intending to pass by, not preoccupied with his disciples or their dangers. He seems not much concerned.

Big storm, straining without success, absence . . . what a set-up for faith!

III

Then they see him. They had not thought to call out for him. This is different from Mark 4 where they wake him up. This time they try to manage the wind themselves. They looked up and there he was. He was there but not recognized. He was in a place and in a form other than habitual. It is like when we see someone out of their normal context, so surprised that we do not recognize them. I would have thought they would have welcomed him. But he scared them. He scared them more than the storm, because in the storm Jesus appears in forms that are not immediately recognizable. He is no good buddy, no nice uncle, no familiar presence. He turns out in the storm beyond their categories. His being there at the edge of the storm with them, moreover, does them no good. He changes nothing . . . until he speaks. Everything depends upon his utterance. The being of Jesus won't do without the self-announcement of Jesus. He has to say something.

He says it: "It is I!" He does not need to say his name. They know it; they had not thought to summon his name or to utter his name or to take the name of Jesus with them. When he said, "It is I," the good exegetes among them recalled all the old cadences of self-announcement made to mothers and fathers in the ancient storm of the exile, also a storm of negation. Jesus speaks the cadences of the God who presides even in the chaos:

> I am YAHWEH, I have called you. (Isa 42:6)

> I am YAHWEH, and besides me there is no savior. (43:11)

> I am He, who blots out your transgressions. (43:25)

> I am the first and I am the last. (44:6)

> I am YAHWEH, who made all things. (44:24)

> I am YAHWEH, and there is no other. (45:5)

That is what he said. The immense counter-power of God is here now in me. The good exegetes know what comes after "I am he, It is I":

> Do not fear!

That is the old, storm-stilling utterance in the faith of our ancestors. That is the word spoken against the storm of exile:

> Do not fear, for I am with you. (Isa 41:10)

> Do not fear, I will help you. (41:13)

> Do not fear, I have redeemed you. (43:1)

> Do not fear, for I am with you. (43:5)

> Do not fear, or be afraid. (44:8)

He said to the same bunch in the storm of Mark 4:40: "Why are you afraid?" Do you not know yet that my utterance is the antidote to the storm? Do you not see that I am the creator of heaven and earth; chaos is interesting to me, but not threat, not a threat to me and therefore not a threat to you.

"Take heart." They had lost heart in their fear, their anxiety, their bewilderment, their panic. Take heart. Take self. Get yourself back. Be who you are. Be who you are. Be who you are and are called to be, because I have addressed you in your chaos out of the oldest cadences of the reliability of the God whom I embody. That is what he said to them.

In that moment, in 6:50, they were with Jesus and in the storm. As Mark tells it, the storm did not quit until v. 51. But in v. 50 he gives his invitation and they must respond then, before v. 51. The space between v. 50 and v. 51, in the text, is only a millimeter, but it is the millimeter in which you gather in an instant all of the options, all the newness. He said to them, "Yes, there is a storm. But I am here. Listen to me. Look at me. Don't heed the storm. Disregard chaos and look at me." They did, in that moment, look at him as the church is always ready to do. But not exclusively. They peeked at the storm still raging. They looked quickly back and forth, back to him in faith, back to the storm in fear. It is like that in the Matthew version that has been escalated (Matt 14:22-33). Peter can manage the water walk as long as he focuses on Jesus and moves toward him. But the text says,

> But when he noticed the strong wind, he became frightened and began to sink.

That is our true situation, is it not, the situation of the disciples, of the church, of us, of the people with whom we minister, while the old order of Western civilization deteriorates. Some welcome the change, many are threatened by it, people not unlike us. Jesus offers to us the *Or* of his complete assurance whereby fear has no credible place. His "Do not be afraid" is a massive invitation to faith, not unlike the parental defeat of a nightmare, who says to the child, "It's all right, I am right here, do not be afraid." Except that unlike a sleeping child, the *Either* of the nightmare around us persists:

> afraid of Babylonian power,
> afraid of selling out,
> afraid of being found out,
> afraid of a failed market, a failed pension, a failed ministry,
>   a failed self.

The *either* evokes us to fear, but the *or* of Jesus defies it. His maneuver works. The wind subsides, having met its match. The storm is defeated; we may take heart and be our true selves in faith once again. Punkt! They are amazed. Of course they are. They are amazed because we tend to overcredit the storm and underestimate the utterance of Jesus. In the calmness of v. 51, they get the point. The storm is powerful, but it cannot prevail or persist in the face of Jesus who wipes out the source of our most elemental anxiety.

IV

Better the story should end in v. 51 with calmness and amazement. But it does not. There is this peculiar v. 52. Surely it is displaced and no doubt blackballed in the Jesus Seminar. In this verse we pay attention to what does not belong in our text. So much better if Mark had not written down what ought not to be there in our story of faith.

"They did not understand about the loaves." The feeding miracle earlier in chapter 6 and its replication to come in chapter 8 are linked in this verse to the storm miracle. It is in the feeding that Jesus uttered the four sovereign verbs of the Eucharist: he took, he blessed, he broke, he gave . . . he fed and had a zillion loaves left over so that grace abounds even as loaves abound. The creation works! The creator is here in abundance. The earth is populated with abundance; the good, generative order of the creation is in effect, not retarded by the traces of chaos that want to defeat generative abundance. They did not understand that the bread of life is thrown into the face of the storm of death, and the bread will win. The bread will win every time.

But they did not get it. They did not get it because they kept one eye on the storm and so lost the freedom of greater truth. They did not get it because he looked like a ghost in his unfamiliar costume as creator. But mostly they did not get it because their hearts were hardened. They had thought they were the emancipated people of the Exodus. But there was so much of Egypt still in them, so much of Pharaoh among them with a hard heart, so much resistance, so much exploitative autonomy, so little capacity to yield in new obedience.

They still were committed to the old order of *either,* the old bondages, the old fears, the old scarcities, the old leverages, that the mystery of "It is I" as yet had no durable authority for them. And so for all their momentary astonishment in v. 51, they are at the end of the narrative as much frightened by the storm as they were at the beginning.

When we include v. 52 as we must, this story narrates us as we are, frightened and having met Jesus, still hardhearted and unyielding. This is not a happy miracle tale, but an exposé of the feebleness of the church where Pharaoh still operates. The story will not lie about us.

But the story does not lie about Jesus either. He is the creator come flesh. He utters the old cadences of the exile-ending creator. He is more than a match for our fear. The storm cannot resist him. The chaos is no force against him. Fear is done in by his Easter, "Do not fear."

The hard news is that this *or* of faith does not easily defeat the *either* of old-fashioned, anxiety-filled storm management. But the good news that I announce to you in the name of the storm-stilling father and the storm-stilling son and the storm-stilling spirit is this. Jesus and his "do not fear" continue to be uttered and will finally utter us beyond our fear. Quit watching the storm and listen!

Academy of Homiletics in Toronto, Ontario / December 4, 1998

On Reading Genesis 12–25

You are a God who awes us and astonishes us.

You are a God who selects a
   dysfunctional family to carry your future.

You are a God who dwells with barren women
   who become mothers in Israel.

You are a God who makes promises with no
   evidence at hand or in sight.

You are a God powerful in purpose,
   hidden in performance,
   faithful over time.

And we are among those drawn into the orbit of
     your life;
  a life teeming with impossibilities
     so hard to trust,
     so impossible to explain,
     so precious to treasure.

Give us this day the freedom to be amazed
   and to trust your way among us,
     even when the world seems closed
      to all futures.

We praise you, future-creating God. Amen.

September 13, 2002

57

A Fourth-Generation Sellout

Genesis 41:11-32, 46-49; 47:13-26; Acts 26:1-3, 12-21

A very strange thing happens in the memory of Israel. In the book of Genesis, things are clear and sequenced about our ancestors. In Genesis 12–24, Abraham with Sarah; Genesis 25–26, Isaac with Rebekah; Genesis 27–36, Jacob with Rachel; and Genesis 37–50, Joseph—four generations of promise. But then Israel reduced this long narrative to a mantra; it comes out in the long form, "the God of Abraham, the God of Isaac, the God of Jacob," or in the short form, "The God of Abraham, Isaac, and Jacob." It is astonishing that in neither long nor short form, does anybody ever say, "the God of Joseph." The guy in the fourth generation of Israel's memory drops out of the mantra. I am going to talk about that dropout and invite you to listen carefully. Because while I talk about Joseph, I may not be talking about him at all, but about someone closer to our own time and place.

I

Joseph is the guy, in the memory of Israel, who had everything, everything his family could give him, and everything that God could give him, through his family and in spite of his family. He was the beloved, long-awaited son of the beloved Rachel, after all of his less wanted half brothers. He was the family pet of whom, when born, his mother exclaimed, "God has taken away my reproach" (Gen 30:23). His very birth is the end of family shame! As the pet he had, as you know, a bright, many-colored coat, emblem to his brothers that his father doted on him. He had a dream, a dream that grew out of the family promise of preeminence from God. He would be first, even as his great-grandfather, his grandfather, and his father had such a promise from God. Beyond these gifts, he is the object of God's providential care. He is protected by God, rescued from the pit and later rescued from an imperial prison. He is a survivor and a winner, much admired in the family story. And beyond all this, he has extrasensory perception, can interpret dreams, has access to secret knowledge, a truly valuable commodity anytime. With such special investment from God, one would imagine we would speak of "the God of Joseph," for this guy had it all, grounded in the richness of his family's faith, ultimate recipient and prize exhibit of this family-protecting God.

II

So what's the problem that Joseph drops out of the theological mantra of Israel? Well, the problem in the narrative is Pharaoh, the cipher in the Old Testament for all that is a threat to Israel's faith and existence. Joseph, for palace hanky-panky, is in prison, but is summoned out of prison by Pharaoh because of his reputation as a dream interpreter. That is, this fourth generation Israelite has intelligence not available in the empire. The foolishness of Israel is wiser than Egyptian wisdom (see 1 Cor 1:25)! Joseph hears the dream of Pharaoh and interprets it . . . his reputation is justified in the empire!

The dream of Pharaoh is a nightmare. He dreams of seven cows fat and sleek, seven cows poor, very ugly, and thin. He tells Joseph, "Never have I seen such ugly cows in all the land of Egypt" (Gen 41:19). No Egyptian academic could explain the nightmare to the king. But the case is easy for Joseph. You dreamed famine! You dreamed scarcity! You dreamed your empire under threat! You have a nightmare that will deconstruct your power.

Joseph proceeds to do more than interpret. He advises. He is a "consultant." Quite quickly, brazenly perhaps, he nominates himself to handle Pharaoh's nightmare of scarcity that will be the undoing of the empire. He becomes the manager and chaplain of the nightmare of the empire.

And then we are told, six chapters later in the narrative, that Joseph acts in his new royal power, to administer the empire in its scarcity. Joseph achieves for Pharaoh, by his rapacious, ruthless wisdom, a monopoly of food that becomes for Pharaoh an economic tool and a political weapon that leverages the Egyptian population (Gen 47:13-20). We are told that in three years:

- Joseph seizes all the money of Pharaoh's subjects, in order to dole out food from Pharaoh's monopoly.

- Joseph confiscates all the livestock of Pharaoh's subjects, in order to dole out food from Pharaoh's monopoly.
- Joseph takes in hock the bodies of Pharaoh's subjects, in order to dole out food from Pharaoh's monopoly, and so reduces citizens to slaves with irreversible economic dependence upon the central economy.

And then the narrative adds laconically:

> So Joseph bought all the land of Egypt for Pharaoh. All the Egyptians sold their fields . . . and the land became Pharaoh's. (Gen 47:20)

Remarkably, through this entire process Joseph does not blink, does not express any compassion or signal any regret or any ambivalence about his harsh actions on behalf of the empire. It is all, as Marlon Brando said in his famous role, "just business." Nor, indeed, does the narrator offer any signal of regret on behalf of Joseph. In the end we do not know if this narrative report is pure admiration for Joseph or if it is quiet irony. We cannot tell, for we get no signal.

III

Joseph senses no moral dilemma in his imperial work. The narrative signals nothing. But Israel's long and wise memory knows, and so drops him from the theological mantra. This Joseph, willed by God's providence and rooted in Israel's oldest, deepest promises has, in these chapters, sold out. He has distanced himself from old covenantal dreams, trading them for the deep nightmare of the empire, sinking deeply into its fear of scarcity.

He might have countered Pharaoh's nightmare with Israel's promise, had he cherished his rootage more. He might have invited Pharaoh out of his phantom of scarcity with the abundance of the land-giving God of Israel. Clearly, however, he holds the old Israelite promises and old Yahwistic abundance loosely, perhaps thinking such old cadences are weak and embarrassing in the environment of the growth economy of Pharaoh. As a consequence, he never utters a word about his own identity, giving himself over completely to Pharaoh's defining nightmare, so compliant to it that he himself might have had disturbing nightmares of scarcity, enacting *imperial power* by day and *imperial threat* by night.

I think he is, in the end, dropped from Israel's theological summary because Israel was unclear about his God. Israel might confess "the God of Joseph" who then turned out to be the Egyptian author of slavery. Joseph had to be dropped because he understood so little and valued so thinly the God of the promise that he served greedy interests that victimized his own people.

At this distance from the narrative, we are left to ponder:

- a tradeoff of promise for nightmare;
- a tradeoff of abundance for scarcity;
- a vocation as manager and chaplain for the imperial nightmare.

It did not need to be so. I have introduced Paul before Agrippa, faith before power, as a counterpoint to Joseph. Paul attests, according to the narrative, "I was not disobedient to the heavenly vision," the vision that got him in a peck of trouble. He was led by his vision to new openness, in trouble with old powers that resisted new vision that craved nightmare but rejected vision. That is Paul who did not yield to the empire, as did Joseph.

The people who hold to the vision and to the promise with courage and steadiness remain in the theological mantra. But there is always a choice between an evangelical vision and an imperial nightmare. Joseph was not a bad man, not especially coerced, more likely seduced, evidently excessively eager, too accustomed to success, and dropped as a sellout in the fourth generation. The tradition is wise and knowing enough in its judgment that it makes one wonder about the fifth and sixth and seventh and umpteenth generations.

Columbia Theological Seminary chapel service / July 14, 2000

On Reading Genesis 25–50

We imagine ourselves self-sufficient
    and then we run short . . .
        short of time,
        short of life,
        short of stamina,
        short of newness.

We find our future closed off and at risk
And we with varying degrees of resolve and determination
        and panic
        and despair
Find ourselves—surprisingly—
      back in your presence,
      waiting instead of acting,
      receiving instead of making
      invited to gratitude instead of success.

We wait and we receive and we thank . . .
 because you are the only Lord of the Future,
    you are the one who births at the eleventh hour,
    you are the one who comes to barrenness
        and makes new,
    you promise like the stars for number
        while we count according to the old math.

You are out beyond us.
We are staggered, stunned, awed.
We did not know you had such futures in you
    and now we know . . . You do indeed! Amen.

September 18, 2002

Misreading the Data

Isaiah 6:9-10; 55:1-3; Mark 8:14-21

Imagine that we are disciples of Jesus, just finishing an intensive seminar with him of a rigorous, demanding action-reflection sequence.

I

The action part of the lesson plan is completed before we get to our text. It was an awesome encounter that reverberates yet among the disciples. The action part of such a learning enterprise is not difficult. You just have to get on the bus, go with the group, and pay close attention. You know Jesus will take care of it all. There is, nonetheless, some anxiety about that part of the learning encounter, because you know that afterward you will be asked hard interpretive questions. You know you will be expected to offer shrewd, insightful interpretations of what you observed, and you know that, contrasted to Jesus, we almost always miss the point, because we are too concrete operational and lack the wild, daring interpretive categories he brings to every "critical incident."

Anyway, recall the action part of the encounter that will bring us to our text. In Mark 6:30-44, Jesus came to a crowd that was like sheep without a shepherd. And while we were watching, before our very eyes, he took a morsel of fish and loaves, fed 5,000, and had twelve baskets of bread left over, enough for every tribe of Israel, enough for everyone in the community. We watched and did not know what to make of it. We were startled beyond explanation.

And then, by way of reinforcement, in Mark 8:1-9, Jesus came to anther crowd, filled as he always was with compassion. He took seven loaves and a few fish. And while we watched, he fed 4,000 hungry people with seven basketsful left, a perfect number of leftovers.

We saw this performance twice. We remembered it. We could smell the bread afterwards and hear the cadences of the event. Both times, we remember, "he took ... he blessed ... he broke ... he gave." That's what he did, twice! Too bad these familiar words have become liturgically reified, because in fact he uttered them in the real world with real bread and real crowds and real hunger and real compassion and real leftovers in abundance. After he did that a second time, we all got on the bus and came home.

II

It came time for the reflection part of the plan. It was a relaxed time, out in a boat, leisurely, but of course intentional. It came time to eat. There was only one loaf of bread. We had forgotten to bring the bread! What had we been thinking? That is what he must have asked himself. He said, "Good grief, did you not know we are in the bread business, the bread of compassion, the bread of new life, the bread for the crowd, the bread of abundance and leftovers, twelve baskets—enough for all—seven baskets—perfect number of leftovers." And we had forgotten! The reflection session did not start very well, because Jesus recognized immediately that we had not computed very well the significance or importance of the action we had twice witnessed.

First, he warned us in a scolding way. Beware the junk food of the Pharisees, reducing nourishment to moral management, the junk food of Herod, reducing nourishment to manipulative power. If you forget the bread of compassion given by Jesus, you will surely be suckered by the bread of manipulation, fear, greed, and anxiety, because neither Herod nor the Pharisees ever has enough. And certainly they never imagine a surplus; they offer only a diet of endless anxiety. That is the alternative to the bread given by Jesus.

Then he began to quiz us, like any good teacher, asking us to process what we had seen in those two encounters. If you look at the transcript of that reflection session, you will see that Jesus' rapid-fire questions remained unanswered. He never paused long enough for us to answer. But perhaps he never intended us to answer. The instruction is the unanswered questions, designed to linger among us, to haunt us to perpetuity.

First, he asked us about *our hearts* that seemed too hard to connect from action to meaningful reflection. Then he asked us about *our eyes* that could not see anything new. Then he asked about *our ears* that could not hear anything important. Then he asked us about *our memory,* and you already know that we had forgotten the bread. His questions are in fact verdicts. Jesus is provoked because we are a dull class that sat through these stupendous actions but computed nothing . . . no sensitivity, no adequate hermeneutical categories, no existential engagement, no transformative discernment.

So like every good teacher, Jesus went back to basics, letting us be safely concrete operational, asking specific questions to which we knew the answers. So he says:

- Back in chapter 6 with 5,000 hungry people, how many baskets of leftovers? We all waved our hands eagerly, "Twelve, twelve, twelve."
- Back at the beginning of chapter 8, with 4,000 hungry people, how many baskets left over?

We had the hang of it now. We were so pleased with ourselves. We shouted the answer confidently, almost in unison: "Seven!" We did not ponder his production of the bread, nor were we amazed at the wonder of transformation from few loaves to many. Rather, we were impressed with our own quick, one-dimensional, uncomprehending knowledge.

And then he said—one of the saddest things he ever said to us in any of his seminars: "Do you not yet understand?" He said, You don't get it, do you? No doubt he wished for better students, for higher standards, for more careful admission policies. We had all the data, but its meaning was well beyond us. We misread the data completely.

III

Why not understand? We are told why in Mark 6:52:

They did not understand about the loaves, because their hearts were hard.

They could not move beyond the concrete operational, because their interpretive sensitivities were dulled. Hard hearts! Any reader hearing that phrase knows that it refers to Pharaoh, the "God-Father" of all hard hearts. Pharaoh is the guy who opposed the God of Israel. Pharaoh is the guy who bought up all the land of the peasants during the famine. Pharaoh is the one who built great storehouse cities with slave labor, because he believed in scarcity . . . never enough . . . get more . . . about to run out. . . . near poor-house lane. His vast wealth and food supply kept increasing; but his heart and ears and eyes were so distorted that he lived in a make-believe world of scarcity where he could not share because he never had enough. The world sponsored and ordered by Pharaoh goes on among us with the abundant leftovers unnoticed.

It eventuates in consumerism, driven by anxiety to more and more commodities, because the world is a fearsome place. The disciples had signed on to the consumer ideology of Pharaoh and Nike and all the grasping cadences of "things." They did not understand the evangelical assertion that the world around Jesus teems with abundance. They missed the messianic declaration that creation is now working well to produce and multiply and be fruitful, enough, more than enough, leftovers for all, abundance, loaves abound. . . . No need to keep, no need to covet, no need to begrudge, because Jesus' fourfold utterance of "take, bless, break, give" is a lordly revamping of the economy. Jesus has effectively, concretely, materially contradicted Pharaoh's economic ideology and shown it to be false. No need for hard hearts that block the truth of the bread. Jesus and his bread miracles cannot be squeezed into an economy of scarcity. The people who "get it" around Jesus—*new hearts, new ears, new eyes, deep memory*—are people who know about the abundance of the new age enacted before our very eyes. We were there when it happened . . . twice.

Since the lordly arrival of Jesus, the new order of the day is generosity, sharing, giving, not fearing, not collecting. Generosity is a way congruent with the way of Jesus who restarts the gifts of creation. Those whose hearts are not any longer Pharaoh-hardened can see the new bread that is the ground of generosity. The cadences of "take, bless, break, give" echo. Midst the words come the sad, hopeful, teasing wonderment, "Do you understand now?" In light of what we have seen and know and trust, the old patterns of Pharaoh, Herod, and the Pharisees are profoundly irrelevant and out of date. The bread business is now all about abundance: Loaves abound! If we watch long enough, even we may understand and act differently, according to the new governance!

Luther Theological Seminary, St. Paul, Minnesota / August 25, 2000

On Enthronement Psalms

We are always watching powers rise and fall.

We watch ourselves,
    noticing how able and capable and vibrant we are,
    and then watching how we are exposed
        as frauds when it counts most.

We watch false claimants all around us:
        tribe,
        nation,
        church,
        product . . .
    and spot quickly the fraud when it counts the most.

We watch and see the world broken open . . .
    in disorder,
    chaos that we cannot bear . . .

And then . . . and now . . . late and sometimes soon,
    we watch your power exercised:
        manifest in great shows of transformation,
        evident in small gestures of healing,
        timidly in night whimpers of presence.

Our Easter zeal runs beyond your frail rule,
Nonetheless we grasp your frail rule,
    chosen over our self-sufficiency that runs out,
    superior to our many idols that lack breath,
    preferred to chaos that is fun only briefly,

We end glad for your rule,
       your rule as painful as Friday,
             as quiet as Saturday,
             as jubilant as Sunday.

       Your rule, our hope,
             our ground of sanity,
             our sense of call,
             or place of life.

Your rule and our responding gratitude. Amen.

October 2, 2002

Disciples of the Great Connector

1 Kings 17:8-16; Mark 12:38-44 / Twenty-Second Sunday after Pentecost

When everything is fixed and settled and closed, cold and jelled, there still occur those odd traces of another truth that may break out, reconfigure, and redefine. For some at least, there is the wistful hope that our story could be retold differently and our lives could be relived differently, outside what is long cold and jelled. In the Old Testament Elijah the prophet is such a trace of retelling and reliving that jolts Israel. He comes among the settled rulers of Israel, the closed assumptions, the eternal power arrangements; he jolts and reconfigures. Our text today is one vignette of his career. Listen to it and notice traces of "another truth" that could break out even in our lives.

I

Elijah lived among kings who managed budgets and worried about taxes, who were committed to notions of scarcity and were swimming in anxiety about the lack of "enough." This fear of scarcity was ordinary for powerful people then as now; they listened to "the numbers" and nervously watched the market fluctuations; they cut every corner and took every advantage, because there is not enough for everyone. "I must, if I can, have my share and part of yours" . . . nothing exceptional about that notion. In our little narrative in 1 Kings 17, the question of scarcity is made all the worse by a drought, an energy crisis with a lack of water, the very scarcity that the king habitually feared.

Into this anxious, fearful scarcity comes Elijah, unintimidated by royal power, unencumbered by royal economics of scarcity, uncontrolled by royal protocol. He is sent by God to this woman who in her despair is about to starve to death. Elisha speaks to her. He speaks to her after all of the settled routines of royal scarcity had nothing to offer her. (In the Bible, always watch what people say; because the ones who speak powerfully and transformatively are the ones who have not settled into the silent woodwork of conformity and despair).

Elijah says to the nameless woman, "Do not be afraid." Imagine saying that to this woman who, with good reason, is about to give up for want of food. His utterance is a startling disruption of her despair. And then he puts substance to his disruptive invitation to move beyond fear:

> The jar of meal will not be emptied and the jug of oil will
> not fail until the day the LORD sends rain on the earth.
> (vv. 13-14)

That is what he said. To the settled economy of anxious scarcity he uttered an absurdity. In the Bible, however, generative people always say what the world thinks is absurd, things like "Do not fear," "Your sins are forgiven, He is risen." Elijah announced a *reliable God-given abundance* to this woman who had nothing and who hoped nothing.

And, we are told, Elisha was as good as his word. For the narrator reports:

> She ate for many days. The jar of meal was not emptied,
> neither did the jug of oil fail, according to the word of the
> LORD. (v. 16)

I told you the saying is odd, even absurd. It is the odd trace of "another truth" that redefines the situation of the woman and of the king and of all the people. It is a miracle! . . . that is, a shattering happening done by God who breaks our assumptions. The miracle is that there is more than enough. There is an overflow of abundance that defies royal scarcity. More than enough, guaranteed by God! The Christian Gospel is a summons to leave the *fearful world of scarcity* and to *practice the world of abundance* in quite concrete ways.

II

Elijah did not just happen on this desperate woman. He was sent there by God; it was his vocation to go be with her. He was dispatched by the God who commissioned him as a prophet. God said to Elijah (and always watch what people say in the Bible):

> Go now to Zarephath which belongs to Sidon and live
> there, for I have commanded a widow there to feed you. . . .

When he came to the gate of the town a widow was gathering sticks for the evening fire.

There she was, just like God said.

Everything in the story is so odd. Elijah was sent beyond the boundaries of his ordinary life. He lived in Northern Israel, not far from the capital city of Samaria. But he is sent away where he had not thought to go.

He is sent to Sidon (what would now be Lebanon), you know, that dangerous place for Jews occupied by Arabs who in turn are dominated by Syria. Go to a strange, dangerous place. Go to a dangerous place occupied by enemies. Break the routine of safety and ordinariness. And in Sidon, go to a village that nobody ever heard of where there are no important people, away from all the media attention.

God's summons moves from the general to the particular, from alien Sidon to the unnoticed village of Zarephath. But then the quite particular . . . a widow there! How odd in the book of Kings to focus on a foreign, unnamed nobody of a woman. How odd in post-election exhaustion concerning school vouchers, Social Security, and Medicare that we meet here to talk about a *nameless* widow from an *unknown* village in *enemy* territory. But then the Bible does that sort of thing to us.

The God of the Bible is like that, a magnet for the ones who drop off of the royal screen. All of our political rhetoric about "working-class families" and "middle-class families," but nothing about a *nameless* widow in an *unnoticed* village in an *enemy* territory, perhaps because she does not vote. The summons to Elijah means to stretch to the limit the capacity of royal Israel to tolerate what God intends, so odd is the intention of God.

- The unnamed woman is a widow . . . without a man in a patriarchal society, without a defender or an advocate, exceedingly vulnerable.
- She is a poor widow . . . no resources, living in a society that has no safety net.
- She has one son, her only social security in a male society, and he is about to die; she is left without resources and without hope. She is ready to die, because she has no viable alternative, dying for want of economic resource.

God sent Elijah to this nobody; God sent Elijah to speak and act abundance for this nobody through a jar that was not emptied and a jug that did not fail. It is enough to ponder God's miraculous abundance that overrides scarcity. It is nearly unthinkable to lodge God's abundance—worldly, material abundance—at the table of this unqualified, unrecognized nobody. But it happened . . . this one time!

> The jar of meal was not emptied, neither did the jug of oil
> fail according to the word of the LORD.

III

The good news this story announces is that in the world where God rules, there is *abundance*. Creation works because the Creator gives in generosity and all who hear this story are invited to step out of the anxious scarcity in which we have all been nurtured. The scandal of this good news is that God's abundance given concretely beyond our expectation, is not designed for the well educated and well connected who live well in lovely, named suburbs like yours and mine; but God's abundance of a quite concrete kind is *aimed toward the lowly,* folks who have no claim upon the wealth of the world except their bodily existence that is an irreducible fact among us.

There is one other point that strikes me. The problem is how to connect *God's abundance* and those who *despair in want.* The odd fact of this story is the connection is not made by God. God sits in the background of the narrative offering directional cues. The connection is made by *a human character* who steps outside his conventional orbit and at great risk mobilizes God's abundance beyond the conventional lines of distribution. The whole is indeed a miracle tale. It is, however, in the end a humanly enacted miracle, the miracle of connecting God's abundance with those who have fallen out of the network.

To be sure, Elijah is a quite peculiar human connector. Just as after him came Jesus of Nazareth, a remarkable and odd human connector who linked the gifts of God to the needs of the world. There were people who gathered around Jesus, odd people who gravitated to him. They are not odd by learning or by pedigree or by endowments or any normal criterion, but odd in that they are *addressed by, available for, and responsive to* the divine intention for the world. The narrative describes that propensity: "according to the word of the LORD that he spoke by Elijah." That is the way the Bible says that *holy stuff* is given over to *human initiative*. That mandate comes from time to time among us. It invites people to be "connectors." It requires that the would-be connectors give up the tired assumptions of the old, failed Kings of Israel, to sign on for a reoriented world of *abundance* for the *vulnerable* by *human connection*. What a mouthful!

It is, we must admit, an odd story. But we come here regularly to hear the odd story again and yet again. Because we yearn to be reassured that the settled, closed world around us, all cold and jelled, is not our full future. There is more and other. We could, as we are ready, put our lives down in the wonder of conviction.

Three lines converge on this day:

1. This is, in many places *Stewardship Sunday,* and we have in the past day been thinking stewardship in this place. But stewardship is not about church budgets. It is about how to care for resources wisely in the midst of the most extravagant wealth the world has ever known. Stewardship is to make connections that the world resists.

2. This is *post-election* with a huge temptation to settle for business as usual for another term, either a little disgruntled or a little relieved . . . except that the need for connection will not wait, not even for four years. And anyway, the people who trust this tale are not overly impressed with settled authority. And so post-election is as good a time as any for new connections humanly made.

3. Finally, the Gospel reading set for this day, about *people of privilege* who devour widows' houses and keep up fine appearances (Mark 12:38-44) contrasts such greedy, fakey folk with the *widow who is a good steward* of her little money. What strikes me in that Gospel story in Mark 12 is Jesus' final instruction:

> All of these have contributed out of their abundance. But
> she out of her poverty has put in everything she had.

Leave it to Jesus to tell it, to combine in the same sentence "abundance" and "widow." Jesus connects *abundance* and *widow*. He is the great connector . . . and we are his disciples in making connections.

Bryn Mawr Presbyterian Church, Bryn Mawr, Pennsylvania / November 12, 2000

On Reading Kings

We have learned the ABCs of power—
        Washington
        Adams
        Jefferson
        Madison
        Monroe
        Adams
        Jackson

The years and the names drone on.

And now we learn the ABCs of power—
        David
        Solomon
        Rehoboam
        Abijah
        Asa
        Jehoshaphat

The names drone and the years and the wars,
    everything settled,
    everything symmetrical
    everything established.

But then comes the intrusion, the disruption, the subversion
    of poets who are uncredentialed,
    of prophets who speak in images and metaphors.

We are staggered along with all power people
    by Elijah and Elisha
    by W. E. B. DuBois
    by Eugene Debs
    by Malcolm X
    by William Sloan Coffin
    by Martin Luther King Jr.
    by loud poets
    and local little protesters.

Disrupted, destabilized, a new chance of peace for war
                of justice for order
                of compassion for law and order.

We don't mind such incursions
    unless it is into our tea party.

We are masters of the drone,
        occasionally recipients of poetry,
    aware, always again aware and at risk,
           knowing your own odd rule that cuts the drone
              and dispatches the poet
              and makes all things new. Amen.

October 4, 2002

What a Difference Mercy Makes

Isaiah 43:16-21; 1 Peter 2:9-10

D id you know that in Western culture, almost all television com-mercials follow the same simple dramatic format?

You have a headache . . . and then you feel good!
    And the difference is aspirin.
You are lonely . . . and then you have friends!
    And the difference is beer.
You are thirsty . . . and then you are satisfied!
    And the difference is Coke, "the Pause that Refreshes."
    You are overweight . . . and then you are slim and attractive,
                                                or lean and mean;
    and the difference is a magic diet formula.

The claim in each case is the same.

I

Did you know that this simple dramatic format is borrowed from the Bible and its good news of salvation?

Once I was lost . . . and now I am found!
    And the difference is the Gospel.
Once I was dead . . . and now I am alive!
    And the difference is Jesus.
Once I was blind . . . and now I see!
    And the difference is the good news of God's love.
Once I was enslaved . . . and now I am free!
    And the difference is God's rescuing mercy.

Our gospel faith is organized around *the way it was* and *the way it is*. And we know the name of the one who has transposed our life from the way it was to the new way it can become. We say that the God known in Jesus Christ has changed everything, and that the television ads are false. They are false because no aspirin or beer, no soft drink or magic diet can give new life. New life is given only by God's miraculous love.

I have taken this theme because the assigned text this morning concerned the transfiguration of Jesus; that is, Jesus took a new form. And then I thought as we move from Epiphany to Lent we may consider the "transfiguration of the church," a new form of life made possible by the Gospel, so that we may think about *the old form of life* and *the new form of life* that God in Christ makes possible among us.

II

This text in 1 Peter 2:9-10 is a very famous text that announces in a rich vocabulary the main truth of the church. The letter is written to a church that is frightened, under threat, and bewildered. The church, in all its bewilderment, is urged by this letter to stand up and be counted as God's people. In lots of places in the U.S. just now, the church is frightened and bewildered, and feels under great threat. And so this letter could be addressed to our own church situation.

The writer does not use much energy on reminding church people of how it used to be, before the coming of the Gospel. You know how it was back then:

> once you had a headache,
> once you were lonely,
> once you were thirsty,
> once you were overweight.

Well, it is worse than that:

Once you were no people. Do you ever think about that? There was a time when there was no community of faith. The people who now constitute the church were not a community, had nothing in common, did not know or trust or belong to each other. It was every person alone, abandoned, helpless.

Once you had not received mercy. There was a time prior to the good news, prior to being called and baptized and loved and forgiven. "Pre-mercy" people are people who must reinvent themselves every day, making themselves up by pressure and achievement and pretense, impressing people, being good enough, being quick enough, being smart enough . . . but of course it is never enough. Because the next day it must be done all over again, until one is exhausted and left in despair. So if you think of ads about lonely people, desolate people, overweight people, frightened people, unforgiven people, think of a *pre*-church, *pre*-gospel, *pre*-mercy, *pre*-life bunch of folk. Once you were no people, once you had not received mercy.

III

And then the miracle! Not beer, not Coke, not diet, not aspirin. The miracle is that Jesus came into the world, gathered up the stranded people and made them into a new community. He called disciples, he called little children, he called publicans and sinners, he called tax collectors and fishermen . . . all sorts of people who did not belong to each other, did not know or trust each other. He drew them all to himself, and in doing so he drew them to each other in a new joy and a new purpose and a new obedience.

We know the tales of Jesus who came among us. Everywhere he came, things were made new. Bartimaeus, the blind beggar, cried out, "Have mercy on me, Son of David." And Jesus had mercy on him; he saw for the first time. He had mercy on him. He extended the healing strength of his life into the need of the beggar and life came there (Mark 10:46-52). Mercy is that strange transformative reach from a center of strength to a center of need that changes everything and makes all things new. The life of Jesus is a sequence of newnesses . . . forgiveness, healing, cleansing, feeding . . . giving life back by the investment of self in others. That is what he did. It is as though the whole world addressed him: "Have mercy on us." He gave his life as a continuing act of mercy. And those who received mercy are formed into a new community. The church is the people who have received mercy.

But we say that this Jesus (who is God's mercy among us) is another wave of mercy, the kind of mercy that God has been doing all through the Old Testament. This is the God who came to needy mothers in the book of Genesis and gave them babies. This is the God who came to the slaves in Egypt and gave freedom. This is the God who—in mercy—gave manna bread in the wilderness and who, in our text from Isaiah, came to the displaced exiles and in mercy did the new thing of bringing them home. In our long story of faith across many generations there are waves and waves of mercy, because God's mercy is given continually in the world and has made all things new. Isaiah has it this way:

This is the LORD who in the past made a way in the sea.

That's the old mercy of Exodus. But now,

Do not remember the former things,
    or consider the things of old.
I am about to do a new thing,
    now it springs forth, do you not perceive it?
I will make a way in the wilderness
    and rivers in the desert. (Isa 43:18-19)

What a difference mercy makes! It is given and present in the memory of the church. It is present and given in our lives today. It is present and given in the world today. Wondrous acts that happen among us to make all things new. Wondrous gifts that open new joy. Next time you watch a TV ad that begins in trouble and ends in well-being, remember, it's not really true! For the "product" will not save and cannot give mercy. What a difference mercy makes, given by the one who is merciful!

IV

Mercy produces something new. It causes to exist that which was not. Jesus caused new people to appear by his self-giving, new people with courage and energy and freedom. Our text describes the new community of the church, those gathered around Jesus in mercy:

You are a chosen race, a royal priesthood, a holy nation . . . God's own people.

You . . . me . . . us! God's own people gathered in mercy! In this place! You see, the church has become so established, so routine, so conventional, so bureaucratic, so institutional that we forget that it is we. The purpose of this text is to speak to the church in its timidity and its anxiety, to say, "You really are somebody!" We are somebody special:

- You are chosen by God, chosen by God to be the new mercy bunch;
- You are a royal priesthood, a priesthood to pray for the whole world, to announce forgiveness to the world, and to enact mercy as a priest might do;
- You are a holy nation, a tribe with a different purpose, drawn from all the nations to this special purpose;
- God's own people, intimately linked to God and God's purposes.

What a mouthful!

And then the text adds:

> In order that you may proclaim the mighty acts of him who called you out of darkness into his marvelous light.
> (v. 9)

"Mighty acts" is a technical term in the Bible. It refers to the whole recital of miracles in the Old and New Testaments. It refers to all the initiatives of mercy that have happened in our past because of God's self-giving.

And here, the sole purpose of the church is to let the world know about the mercies that are still to happen:

- to declare that no trouble is beyond the reach of God's mercy;
- to declare that a technological world is not closed to God's good mercy;
- to declare that no quarrel or dispute is beyond God's reconciliation;
- to declare that no abandonment leaves one so helpless that God cannot help in mercy.

What a mouthful, especially in a technological society where we think things are closed off, where we are attempt to live as though there were no mercy.

I think much of the church has lost its way. We worry about rules, and morality, worry about members and dollars, worry about culture wars and church splits, worry about imposing our way on others in order to get everyone in the right on morality or doctrine or piety or liturgy . . . all as though we have not received mercy.

Listen to this:

> Once you had not received mercy,
> and now you have received mercy.

That's all. That's everything. That's what the world in its desolate anxiety does not know. God is not a hypothesis or a good idea, but an agent who turns what was into what will be. The good news is the new act of mercy God is always yet again doing. And we get to tell it and to show it! We get to tell it and show it because we are God's own people, a new people with a new purpose, the one for which the world waits, even as the world falls apart in greed and anger and anxiety. Mercy is God's response to us, and then through us and beyond us. It's a big difference!

Memorial Presbyterian Church, St. Augustine, Florida / February 25, 2001

On Reading Psalm 2

Creator in power,
protector in sovereignty,
giver of life in generosity,
Spawner of every fish,
Hen to every bird,
bearer of every beast of the field:
     "goodness" you give
     "goodness" you say
     "goodness" you guarantee . . .

And we receive—in need like all creatures
     in gratitude like all creeping things
     in obedience like every glad plant.

"Very good" at the break of day—"good" indeed!
     And in that very instant: violence!
          oppression!
          explosion!
          blood, tears!
          frantic running, desperate shouting!
          anxious huddling in loss!

And we are double-minded:
     awed by you, distracted by dysfunction;
     trusting in you, bothered beyond focus;
       at ease in Sabbath, deeply diseased.

"Very good" . . . very scary . . . very vulnerable:
     Praise to you . . . and a doubt

exaltation toward you . . . and weary hope
all offered to you, creator God, before whom we bow . . .
stiffly. Amen.

June 18, 2002 (Montreat)

Newness from God that Unlearns Family

John 13:31-35; Acts 11:1-18; Revelation 21:1-6 / Fifth Sunday of Easter

Peter is the key character in this story in Acts, and he is in a deep crisis. In order to understand his crisis, we do well to consider the longer sweep of his life. We meet him first as a fisherman. We notice that when the disciples are in a discussion, he always speaks first; he no doubt became the leader of the early church, so that he is remembered by tradition as having been the first Bishop of the church in Rome, that is, the first pope.

I

We really know nothing about his younger years; we have some hints and can imagine the rest. On this Mother's Day, we can imagine that he was a family man who dearly valued his family. We are told only of his mother-in-law. But he had a mother, and she surely had him circumcised in good order. He grew up to be a good Jewish boy in a good Jewish family that kept a kosher kitchen. He kept to all the disciplines that his religious tradition had taught him. The crisis of our text comes when Peter has a dream that threatens everything he was taught in his family and by his mother.

I suggest that this man Peter is very much like most of us who grew up in good families where our mothers love us and we love our mothers. And it is the way we grow our own children and watch carefully over our grandchildren. We teach our children the passions and commitments of our family, what we value, how we see things, what we trust, what we care about, how we live. We do what we can to tell our kids why we are a different kind of family, and why we think differently about money and TV and sex, and so on and on. And our kids believe us . . . until they spend that first night at a friend's house and discover that another family does it all very differently. Until that moment they had assumed that the way our family did it was the right way, that everyone lived just like us. No wonder a little child gets weepy at bedtime the first night away from home, yearning for what is reliable and familiar, weeping at what is strange and new that is seen to be very upsetting.

II

Peter was a church leader upon whom everyone counted to be reliable and orthodox and safe. Of late, he had been acting strangely and his best friends in the church had noticed. They had seen him eating with a Roman soldier named Cornelius, and they knew that Cornelius, because he was a Roman soldier, was not circumcised. Such a man as Cornelius may have been a good man, but he is "not one of us." He is excluded from table fellowship with Jewish Christians who still kept the rule of a kosher kitchen and attended to what was proper and clean and holy for the people of God. To violate those norms would endanger the entire community. So they quizzed Peter in a tone of accusation.

Peter explains to his church friends why he has undertaken this new behavior that seems odd, shocking, and dangerous. He says, I was resting one day and fell into a trance; we would call it a dream. The dream might be a fantasy, but they took it as a word from God, an interruption in his safe life with a new truth given when one's guard is down. In the dream, there came down from heaven a large sheet holding a bunch of snakes and birds. And a voice in the dream said to Peter, "Rise and eat." Have a snake sandwich and a bird salad.

But Peter could not do it. He could not obey and eat a snake, because his Jewish mother had taught him that snakes are "unclean" and birds are profane; to eat them would violate his self-understanding as a person of faith who kept within the bounds of community practice. Peter had ringing in his ears the old rules from his mother and from his synagogue instruction and from the old Torah:

> These you shall regard as detestable among the birds. They shall not be eaten; they are an abomination: the eagle, the vulture, the osprey, the buzzard . . . These are unclean for you among the creatures that swarm upon the earth: the weasel, the mouse, the great lizard, the gecko, the land crocodile. (Lev 11:13-14, 29-30)

Do not eat them! So Peter said, in the trance to the voice from heaven:

I cannot eat that snake. My mother told me not to eat it. I
have never had anything profane or unclean in my mouth.

And the voice of heaven said to him:

What God has made clean you must not call unclean.

Peter and the voice from heaven had that same exchange three times.
"No," said Peter. "Yes," said the voice. And then Peter knew that he
was to meet with this uncircumcised non-Jew, Cornelius, and eat with
him. He had been taught, from little on, that such people are contam-
inating; and now God breaks that notion and makes new fellowship
possible across old lines.

III

Now I think it is purely accidental (or providential!) that this text
turns up in the lectionary on Mother's Day, because the Lectionary
committee pays no attention to Mother's Day, a day that is not in the
church year. Rather, this day is "the Fifth Sunday of Easter." But since
we have this text, consider this. The crisis Peter faced was that he
learned in that moment of trance, in which God spoke to him afresh,
that he had to move beyond his faith tradition learned from his family.
He had to break free of what his family had taught him. He had to face
the fact that what his mother told him, the best she knew, was no
longer adequate. He had to unlearn some of his tradition, unlearn his
family, unlearn his mother, to discern that the distinctions of "us and
them," of clean and unclean, of Jew and Gentile, in the large mercy of
God is simply wrong. It is no wonder that he was in a deep crisis. It is
no wonder that the other Jewish Christians who trusted him recognized that he had done something strange that opened their new faith
in ways that shocked them deeply.

In this case, it is a discovery that Jewish rules are broken by the
Gospel so that the church is opened to Gentiles; in this narrative the
church is transformed into a worldwide church, never to be the same
again. It is like that with everyone who meets Jesus and is addressed
by the Gospel. Everyone has to face the crisis that God's love and
God's care for the world is large and expansive and beyond our usual
horizons. Everyone has to learn, in the power of the Gospel, that
while our traditions and our families and our mothers did the best

they knew, the rules in the family tend to be small and fearful, not nearly big enough or bold enough for God's love of the world. Thus on Mother's Day we remember and give thanks for our mothers. And then we face the truth that we must unlearn some of what they taught us in order to meet Jesus and to enter into God's fuller purpose for our lives.

This unlearning and relearning is an endless process. Paul writes:

There is no longer Jew or Greek,
there is no longer slave or free;
there is no longer male or female,
for all are one in Christ. (Gal 3:28)

This story about Peter is the story of discovering that in Christ there is no Jew or Greek, and any old rule that makes that distinction between clean and unclean must be unlearned. About "slave and free," we have had a hard time, beyond the ending of slavery, we still struggle with racist distinctions of black and white or Asian or Hispanic. As Peter dealt with Cornelius the Roman soldier *eating,* so the measure of "slave or free" was a question at the lunch counters we can still remember and the resulting "table fellowship." Of late, moreover, we are in a struggle about "male and female," about sexual differentiations and who gets in and all of that. It is the same issue one more time, the same issue that always surfaces in God's large love, the same issue about unlearning what our family taught us, because some of it is not true. That fact hits us here and there, in a dream, in a trance, in a prayer, in a thought, and we are shaken to move into God's newness.

V

In the book of Acts we remember the crisis when the early church was led by God's Spirit into a large world that seemed strange and threatening, and there to trust Jesus in new, deeper ways. The reason that is so important to us now is that the church in our society is being led to newness, new awarenesses, new duties, new forms of mission, new neighbors, new possibilities that are not easy for us, that frighten us and make us defensive. In many ways we want to keep things the way they used to be, to be the way the tradition said it was, and the way our mothers taught us it should be. But comes the voice in a dream to assure us that we will be safe in a new place. And so the voice says,

"Take and embrace" what you thought was scary and forbidden. And so we are told that when Peter explained the newness to his friends and all that he had unlearned, it was a "message by which your entire household will be saved" (v. 14). We are told, moreover, that God's Holy Spirit—a spirit of joy and power and well-being—came upon them (v. 15), and they began to praise God (v. 18).

Our theme is God's newness that causes us to unlearn so much, because we now see more clearly and love more dearly. We Christians are people open enough to be led by Christ to newness. That newness from God reaches its fullest articulation in this statement of Jesus that we read in the assigned lesson from the Fourth Gospel:

> I give you a new commandment, that you love one another. Just as I have loved you, you also should love one another. By this everyone will know that you are my disciples, if you have love for one another. (John 13:34-35)

That, of course, is what good mothers have always taught. But with little children, the invitation to love tends to be circumscribed and limited by fear and caution. So love one another . . . in the family, in the neighborhood, in the church, but kids pick up the secret message that this horizon of love is narrow and does not really refer to everyone.

> So love everyone, but be careful strangers.
> So love all Presbyterians, but be careful of Baptists.
> So love all Christians, but watch out for Muslims,
>   etc., etc., etc., until we mostly love our own kind.

Jesus makes it clear and simple, as he is about to leave his disciples. The accent is on what is new. This is a new command that runs beyond the familiar ten commands. A brand new commandment is given that runs beyond the tradition, and our families and our mothers. Peter was commanded to love the Roman centurion who he was taught was unclean. As the world becomes smaller and resources become more limited, society becomes more fearful and violent and destructive. And the people of Jesus are put down in the middle of it, to counter the power of hate and anger and exclusion, to see that God's arms of love are large like the arms of the mothers who held us. The reason to move to the new commandment is to get in sync with what God is doing in the world. God is, even as we speak, fashioning a new world of embrace and well-being that requires no barriers of exclusiveness. So it is written in the last promise of the Bible, in the book of Revelation:

> See, the home of God is among mortals.
> He will dwell with them as their God;
> they will be his peoples,
> and God himself will be with them;
> he will wipe every tear from their eyes.
> Death will be no more;
> mourning and crying and pain will be no more,
> for the first things have passed away.
>
> And the one who was seated on the throne said, "See, I am making all things new." (Rev 21:3-5)

All things new . . . God in our presence, no tears, no death, no pain . . . all things new. And our part is a new commandment. That's a push beyond most of our mothers. But our mothers, after they had taught what they could, would have wanted us to move on to embrace God's newness. Our life in the church would be greatly different if Peter had resisted the dream of newness. But he did not resist. And we do not resist it either, as we move to God's love of which our mothers' love was a precious hint.

St. Charles Avenue Presbyterian Church, New Orleans, Louisiana / May 13, 2001

On Reading Joshua and Judges

Sometimes we feel like a motherless child,
Sometimes we feel like a fatherless orphan,
Sometimes we feel like a landless refugee,
Sometimes we feel like we belong in no sure place.

      We yearn,
      we hope,
      we weep,
      we wait.

And many others yearn and
          hope and
          weep and
          wait along with us—
               more motherless than are we,
               more orphaned than are we,
               more refugees than are we,
               more homeless than are we.

We . . . and they . . . cling to promises and entitlements.

      Even when we are well settled and tenured and entitled,
          we still cling
          and our clinging produces other
               orphans and other refugees.

Oh God of all the homeless . . .
      give land and home and *shalom,*
      correct our over-homefulness,
      and redistribute land among all the orphans.

Stop all land grabs including ours,
        and give gifts again according to need,
           according to your lavish generosity. Amen.

September 27, 2002

One Exorcism, One Earthquake,
One Baptism . . . and Joy

Psalm 97; Acts 16:16-34; Revelation 22:12-21 / Seventh Sunday of Easter

In the life of the church, this is an odd and special Sunday: It is the final, seventh Sunday of the Easter season; seven Sundays is a long time to stay fixed on the wonder of the resurrection, that defining miracle of new life given us in Jesus.

It is the Sunday just after Ascension, when the church celebrates the ascent of Jesus to power, as we confess him who "sits at the right hand of God the Father, from where he will come to judge the living and the dead."

It is the Sunday preceding Pentecost, when the church remembers, celebrates, and anticipates God's gift of new spirit into the church to power us to new obedience.

This is a Sunday when all these matters converge: resurrection / ascent to power / spirit. In my church in the UCC and in the common lectionary, the reading assigned for today from the book of Acts is a very strange one indeed. I imagine the lectionary committee sitting and thinking, "Let's find the oddest, most outrageous text we can find"—which, like the sequence of resurrection, ascent to power, Pentecost—blows away all our conventional categories by which we make sense of our lives. This text in Acts 16 does just that. It consists in three episodes.

I

First, in verses 16-18, there is an exorcism. There was a young girl who was hired by pimps to perform her curious gifts of the spirit that opposed the early church. She might have represented gnosticism or New Age religion or some such alternative to the Gospel; she critiqued the church by saying that the Christians were too much enslaved to a single God, Most High God, who did not allow for all kinds of more open and inclusive religious sensibilities.

95

Paul could not bear her critique and is rather hard-nosed toward her. He decides to deal with the slave girl who was being used by accusing the early church of being enslaved by its faith. The slave girl is not wicked, but she is possessed. And Paul says to the possessing spirit:

> I order you in the name of Jesus of Nazareth to come out
> of her. (v. 18)

The destructive spirit obeyed Paul: It came out! It came out "in that very hour."

Now we can get hung up on the exorcism that sounds weird to people like us in mainstream Christian faith. But take it another way. Take it as ascension. Jesus has come to power; the one crucified and risen now has all the powers of heaven and earth in obedience, so that even this hostile spirit obeys the command given in the name of Jesus.

When we transpose that strange event to our own lives, each of us has a place, large or small, where we act against our true selves. We are like the slave girl who attacks the one who can emancipate her. The good news given in this strange narrative is that the name and the person and the rule of Jesus let us become our true selves, not possessed, not occupied, not driven, not anxious. The good news is that the crucified/risen one lets us be our true selves, without any of the fever or paralysis or pathologies of the day that are everywhere.

II

The enactment of the power of Jesus—who now reigns in full authority—evokes hostility from those who refuse the freedom he gives. In this case, hostility to the emancipation for the slave girl comes from the pimps who used her to make money. As usual, the deep theological crisis of this narrative shows up in a simple dispute about money. There is money to be made in a thousand enslavements—whether drug addiction or consumerism or whatever—and there is no money to be made in a genuine evangelical act that refuses being a huckster.

The pimps are really angry at the loss caused by the freedom that Jesus has given the slave girl. As a result, they take Paul and Silas to court and accuse them of disturbing the social peace. Well, of course, people who practice emancipation and permit people to become their true selves always rock the boat, always upset the skewed order of oppression and repression. The magistrates hear the case and join in the anger of the crowd; official power and angry street power act together to restrain the freedom given through Jesus. That surely is a second learning in this dramatic narrative after we have learned about the power of Jesus to set free. To enact the freedom of Jesus in the real world upsets settled social arrangements. Christians who act in such a way are dangerous people who take on risks and who pay costs that arise with the Gospel. The official order given by the court against the Christians seeks to curb the revolutionary upset of the church:

> After they had given them a severe flogging, they threw
> them into prison and ordered the jailer to keep them
> securely. Following these instructions, he put them in the
> innermost cell and fastened their feet in the stocks.
> (vv. 23-24)

III

Now Paul and Silas were in jail as disturbers of the peace. They were locked up, but, says the narrative, they stayed free. They prayed and they sang hymns and, we are told, the other prisoners listened to them with fascination. They were busy transforming the prison, turning it into a revolutionary community, suggesting that the powers of restraint were no match for the freedom of Jesus: what a mouthful!

But there is more. That same night, suddenly, there was an earthquake. Does anybody, anybody here, think that the earthquake was an accident? Do you think anyone in that prison thought it was a coincidence? The narrator does not say so, but surely the earthquake was the work of the Easter God, the ascended God, acting to overturn yet another institution of enslavement:

> Suddenly . . . the foundations of the prison were shaken;
> and immediately all the doors were opened and every-
> one's chains were unfastened. (v. 26)

The jailer panicked; he thought he was guilty of neglect of duty, assuming everyone had escaped on his watch.

But of course, these early Christians were not ready to escape when they had the chance. They were in the trouble and they stayed there, even with chains gone and doors opened. The jailer recognized immediately that more than an earthquake had happened. He understood that the earthquake was connected to these odd singing, praying Christians who did not flee.

> The warden asked the prisoners, "What shall I do to be saved?" (v. 30)

Paul answered, the same Paul who had commanded the spirit to leave the slave girl:

> Believe on the Lord Jesus and you will be saved.
> (v. 31)

They were baptized. They shared a wondrous moment, jailer and prisoners, engaged together in an odd moment of freedom, baptized into the truth and freedom of the Gospel.

IV

Now I know that this story has nothing to do with you, as it really has nothing to do with me:

- casting out a troublesome spirit;
- jailed for disturbing the peace;
- saved by an earthquake and baptized as a new believer.

But then: Easter has nothing to do with us either;
    Ascension has nothing to do with us either;
    Pentecost has nothing to do with us either.
Unless there is a hope and a yearning,

> unless wanting to be free like the slave girl was freed,
> unless fearful like the magistrates who joined the crowd;
> unless asleep like the jailer, suspecting nothing,
> unless listening to the singing and praying like the other
>   prisoners,
> unless at the edge of an earthquake and fearful.

If any of this comes close to your life, then this matters,

- that a slave girl was made free to be herself;
- that testimony led to risk;
- that a jail opened miraculously to those singing and praying.

And all of that is encompassed in the narrative by the two mantras of the name of Jesus. At the beginning in verse 18, said to the spirit in the slave girl:

> I order you in the name of Jesus Christ to come out of her.

At the conclusion in verse 31, to the jailer:

> Believe on the Lord Jesus, and you will be saved, you and
> your household.

At the beginning and at the end, unsuspecting, powerless, hopeless people are invited to begin again, to gather around the power of God that is given in Jesus, that will be given endlessly in the spirit, a power that breaks old bondages, that crushes old killing arrangements, that opens old doors long kept closed.

It is no wonder that we have Psalm 97 for this Sunday, for it sings of God's ascent to power:

> The LORD is king! Let the earth rejoice;
>   let the many coastlands be glad!
> Clouds and thick darkness are all around him;
>   righteousness and justice are the foundation of his throne.
> Fire goes before him,
>   and consumes his adversaries on every side.
> His lightnings light up the world;
>   the earth sees and trembles.
> The mountains melt like wax before the LORD,
>   before the Lord of all the earth . . .
> Light dawns for the righteous,
>   and joy for the upright in heart.
> Rejoice in the LORD, O you righteous,
>   and give thanks to his holy name! (vv. 1-5, 11-12)

All of these festival days—Easter/Ascension/Pentecost—are attempts to enact a newness that is an inexplicable gift from God.

> Nobody knows how the slave girl got free;
> Nobody knows how the earthquake came;
> Nobody knows how the prison was opened.

But they noticed that the people who lived that way referred their lives back to Jesus. And the new ones wanted to refer their lives in new ways to Jesus. That is what baptism is about . . . referring our lives to Jesus,

> being free,
> singing songs,
> praying prayers,
> watching earthquakes,
> being unafraid and filled with joy.

In the narrative, the Christians have no access to the pimps or the magistrates or the jailer. Well, at the last moment, the jailer reached out for newness and joined their new joyous way in the world. He had to decide afresh and unafraid. So do we all.

John Knox Presbyterian Church, Dunedin, New Zealand / May 27, 2001

On Reading Psalm 5

We know about pits and snares and depths.
We know about silence and absence and abandonment
    and helplessness.
We know about passionate petition and eager insistence,
        but we also know about the silence of shame,
        the darkness of guilt,
        the terror of resentment.

We know about the long night out of control in anxiety,
          when we are our true selves even if not our best selves.

We also know, some of us often,
        many of us seldom,
        all of us sometime,
    about the break of day when night is broken,
          when speech cracks silence,
          when your compassion overrides our shame,
          when your healing mercy vetoes our hurt,
          when your massive forgiveness overrides our
            resentment.

We do not know how it is that you break the night.
We do not know why it is that you harvest our silence into presence.
We only know—like many mothers and fathers—
        that in the long nights you hover until daybreak
        and we find that every new dawn is Easter yet again.
We know the concession speech made by Death:
        "He is not here, He is risen."

We are astonished that you break the night with risenness.
In our timidity we trail your risen self;
We find ourselves, now and then, Eastered alongside you.
We flex our muscles and with you find ourselves stronger than
the night.
We are astonished—and glad!

We say you and tell you, praise you and obey you, all the day long,
unafraid of the night that will surely come soon again. Amen.

June 21, 2002 (Montreat)

The Stunning Outcome of a
One-Person Search Committee

1 Kings 19:19-21; 2 Kings 2:9-15; Luke 9:59-62

The work of some search committees is long, complicated, and quite public, surrounded by many rumors and much intrigue. There are other search committees that operate quickly, quietly, and simply, rather like the Westminster Dog Show—one judge looks and points to the winner, and the dogs do not even know the process is going on. The case of Elijah as a search committee is of the latter type. His decision is quick and terse, so terse that he does not say anything. He finds Elisha doing fieldwork (with twelve yoke of oxen!) and he throws his mantle over him. The choice is decisive; the deed is done irreversibly, and Elisha knows it:

> Let me kiss my father and my mother, and then I will
> follow you. (1 Kgs 19:20)

No discussion, no negotiation, no terms of call.

For these days, I have had search committees on my mind, as had Elijah. Be assured, I am not thinking here of the search for a president that ended happily with Laura Mendenhall. No need to talk about that, for it is a done deal and we are all elated. Out of this text, rather, I imagined the great ATS Accrediting Agency in the sky consisting in One Person—or Three Persons in one substance, depending on how one counts—conducting a search for just one responsive seminary. I imagined that the search is quick and quiet and simple, so that most do not know the search is underway. Imagine just now, just today, just in our imagination that search committee is eyeing this seminary, anticipating that this might be the one for the coming days of mission. And if the Search Committee in the sky reaches such a conclusion, then it will of course accord with what many of us think anyway, that this seminary is the one for the coming days of mission.

Elisha's response to Elijah's search decision is quick and short and to the point. He says, "I will follow you." I am ready. I just need to do three quick things, and then I will follow without reservation:

1. He wraps the mantle tight around his body, the palpable sign of God's summons, to see how it feels and how it fits, to be reassured that there was a workable match between the call and the mantle or alternatively, as we say, to see if for him there was a convergence of "deep gladness and the world's deep need."

2. He wanted to go home and kiss his mom and dad. Maybe he wanted their permission. Maybe he wanted them to appreciate and affirm his high calling. Or perhaps he was frightened enough that he did not want to soar off into newness without firm rootage. He did not slough off his parents but he valued them. It occurred to me that the seminary picked by the great Accrediting Agency for the new season of mission in the twenty-first century better kiss parents and ancestors, better touch the past, better treasure the heritage, better remember the best hopes and dreams all the family has entertained before now. And I imagine, as was said about Abraham Heschel when he left his Jewish ghetto in Poland and went off to study in Berlin, that he had a two-way ticket and must have often returned to kiss his mother and father, for what is asked of him now is connected to what is old and treasured.

3. He took the twelve yoke of oxen with which he was plowing (he was like most CTS folk, quite upper middle class). He killed and butchered them and had a great feast. Everyone in the village was so excited about his call that they lavished their endowment on the future. No keeping back ten or eight or six or even two oxen for a rainy season; the feast to mark a time of glad obedience must be extravagant, no parsimony when the search committee acts.

And then says the narrator: He set out to follow Elijah:

- test the call with the mantle;
- embrace the tradition with a kiss;
- lavish the endowment on the future.

And then, in the next episode, he watched Elijah ascend. He pled with Elijah:

Please let me inherit a double portion of your spirit.

I take it he means the Spirit of God that had infused Elijah. He knew what he needed. He needed the "force of God" for the dangers ahead, the force that would matter decisively,

> after he had tested the call with the mantle;
> after he had embraced the tradition with a kiss;
> after he had lavished the endowment on the future.

He needed more than he could control or enact. He needed a gift from God.

He picked up the mantle, now ready. He struck the water of the Jordan; and it parted! He did a new Exodus like Moses, what we used to call "God's mighty deed in history." The community of supporters gathered around him. They were shrewd observers, like an ordination commission, and they said:

> The spirit of Elijah rests on Elisha.

Search process completed!

He asked for a double portion and he received it. And he never looked back! He was blown by the wind into places he had never thought to go, to enact things he had never thought to do. Now I know this is just an inaugural festival; it is not a Pentecost. But notice that "following" creates the conditions whereby the "force" is given that moves the nominee into a new range of activity, into a future radically different from his past.

III

Then follows the work of the wind through this Elisha. The future is given in Israel through this mantle-wearing, parent-kissing, oxen-butchering, wind-blown disciple.

1. The spirit propels this called one into a concrete *economic situation of poverty and scarcity* (2 Kgs 4:1-7). He met up with a widow whose life was to be shut down by a creditor. The narrative uses specifically economic terms of "creditor/debtor," and Elisha plunges into the middle of the crisis. He overwhelms the hapless widow with oil, that most precious commodity. All the neighbors bring their pots

and pans; the oil keeps running, because it takes a village to receive all the new gifts. In the end, the woman pays all her debts and can live again. The narrator does not ask how this happened; but the answer would have been, a double portion of the spirit!

2. The spirit pushed the candidate to commit *an overt ecumenical act,* a ministry outside his well-defined Israel (2 Kgs 5:1-19). Naaman, the Syrian general, grudgingly comes to Elisha with leprosy, and he is healed. So Jesus remembers:

> There were also many lepers in Israel in the time of the prophet Elisha, and none of them was cleansed except Naaman the Syrian. (Luke 4:27)

The healed general offers to pay for the healing, and Elisha refuses. Then the general apologizes to the prophet and says, "You know, I am a political general, and when I return home, I will be in a media event in the cathedral, worshiping Rimmon, a God other than the one that has healed me." Elisha, great ecumenist that he is who anticipates later pluralism, says to him, "Shalom, go in peace," that is, "never mind."

3. The prophet who succeeds Elijah is dispatched by the spirit *into the world of death,* there to enact God's gift of life (2 Kgs 4:32-37). He had given to the Shunammite woman a son, and then he died. The mother of the dead son has complete confidence in Elisha, and so the prophet goes to the dead boy, prays, breathes mouth to mouth with the *ruah*, and the boy lives. The narrative lets us see that this double-portioned carrier is an Easter force for life in a world where the power of death is vibrant and pervasive. In the narrative, life will win, carried by the prophet.

4. The prophet is led by the Spirit to an *intimate pastoral crisis where there is a lack of food* (2 Kgs 4:42-44). That lack signifies that God's creation is not fully functioning. There is such a mismatch of need and resources, only twenty loaves of barley, and then abruptly he feeds them. The bread is passed under his double spirit; we are told that a hundred people ate. They ate and had some left, according to the word of the Lord. This act, so laden with Eucharistic thickness, of course anticipates the feeding Jesus will do.

These acts constitute an amazing catalogue of transformative miracles:

- an economic intervention that redresses the life of creditors and debtors;
- an overt ecumenical act that values those unlike "us";
- an Easter foray into the sphere of death to bring life;
- a pastoral feeding, bespeaking the generosity of the Creator.

No doubt all of these stories are designed to celebrate and enhance this remembered figure of power who had *a cloak, a kiss, a festival,* and worked in awesome ways to make things new. No doubt all the stories, theologically self-conscious, witness to God's governance in the large and small places of the world where it was thought they were autonomous. In truth, these stories are not simply about God's governance or simply about the oddness of the prophet, but about the *strange, unfamiliar convergence of human agency and divine sovereignty allied for a newness* that the world had not yet imagined. The stunning outcome of this search process was the release of power for life in a world weary with the gap between creditors and debtors, exhausted with faith turned in on itself exclusively, despairing in the face of the power of death to which there seemed no antidote, fed up with so many little children to feed and not enough bread. We are treated here to no explanations, but only a terse summons, a rush of energy, God's power for life given concrete, fleshly form. We are brought up short before the power for life that is so unspeakable that when Elisha dies several chapters later they threw another dead body into his grave with his body, and that one came alive when it touched the still bones of Elisha (2 Kgs 13:20-23). This double-portioned man continues, it is said, to be a force for life even in his own death. Of course this is all legend. It is remote from us. It is personal and not institutional, spun by the spirit and not at all decent and in order. It has, surely, nothing to do with us. Except we never know with a *cloak* and a *kiss* and *oxen butchered,* and the force sent anew.

IV

You will notice I have not yet come to the Gospel reading. As usual Jesus is more radical than the antecedents in Israel. Elijah let his designee go kiss his mother and father. Jesus said, "Forget about them." Jesus seems to call to a more radical break, no time to go home first. But the cases are not quite parallel. Evidently Elisha's mother and father are alive and well, functioning and supportive of this new place where deep gladness and the deep need of the world converge. In the second case, the father is already dead. In that case the demand is sharper: Do not go back to death. Do not kiss a corpse.

It occurred to me that when the great Accrediting Agency in the sky points, one task for the designee is to sort out vibrant, pertinent antecedents and failed antecedents that will give no life. Jesus' word is, do not spend energy on failed antecedents, but unload them to travel light in obedience.

Perhaps:

- leave off old memories that are small and suffocating;
- leave off old speeches that seem to need one more utterance in one more meeting;
- leave off pet projects whereby an incidental has become definitional;
- leave off old hurts and affronts that are revisited too often to permit healing;
- leave off the shrillness that always needs to make one more "statement";
- leave off old fears and hates and angers that block the wind, old modes of doctrine (liberal or conservative) that are only cultural accidents, and old moralities (liberal or conservative) that are in fact disguised fear and vested interest.

The one he addressed was ready, but sad:

I will follow you Lord; but let me first say farewell to those at my home.

Jesus, however, is an impatient search committee:

None who puts a hand to the plow and looks back is fit for the kingdom of God. (v. 62)

So imagine a Search Committee dreaming of the coming governance:

- we with a cloak of emancipated responsibility;
- we with vibrant mothers and fathers to embrace and failed mothers and fathers to relinquish;

- we with twelve oxen or more, but not finally dependent on market fluctuations;
- propelled into economic situations of creditors and debtors;
- pushed into ecumenical contexts, healing among those who are long-time outsiders and alien to us;
- dispatched into a world where death is strong, in order to enact gestures of new life;
- led into intimate places of need to feed and house and clothe, with as many as twelve baskets left over.

Seminaries like ours are mostly equipped for the steadiness of twentieth-century denominational patterns. And now comes the twenty-first century and the purposes of God in, with, under, and beyond all the structures and categories and procedures comfortable and familiar to us.

The Search Committee, so says the text, is able to find a candidate ready to be propelled, pushed, dispatched, led, summoned to the places where "deep gladness and deep need" converge. It is hard to measure the gift of the Spirit about to be given among us. But it is, we surmise, doubled in joy and with names written in heaven. Doubled is a lot. More than enough!

Columbia Theological Seminary / April 25, 2001
in connection with the inauguration of President Laura Mendenhall

On Reading Psalm 4

Oh for a thousand tongues, thousand and thousand,
>to sing our amazement at the break of day,
>to sing our awe that we are, because you utter us,
>to sing our gratitude that life breaks so well among us,
>to sing old, old songs that we have loved so well,
>to tell the old, old story
>>that becomes the new, new song as fresh and urgent
>>as today.

Such tongues you give us—and some sing . . .
>but some among us today
>>and many of us often, and
>>all of us sometimes,
>refuse such tongue, grow silent as teenagers,
>>>grow resentful as a hurt child,
>>>grow as calculating as those near defeat . . .

>And cannot sing anything of amazement, awe, or gratitude,
>>cannot hear old songs or old stories, and resist new songs
>>>because our tongues first must come to truth
>>>>about our hurt that is deep,
>>>>about our fear that is massive,
>>>>about our hate that is torrid,
>>>>and about our alienation that is thick.

Some among us today,
>and many of us often,
>>and all of us sometimes
>>>are silenced too long, as though our life were a
>>>shushed library
>>>>where we can die in silence.

Our words hover close to utterance but not out,
    and muteness reigns—
        tongues unused, words unuttered, silence unbroken.

And some find permit, license to tell the truth of empty void,
                           shushed self-esteem,
                           doubted healing.

All out, all said, all risked
    And we dare to know—for sure—
        that for all our able tongues

            You have *ears*:
              You listen
              You heed
              You invest
              You care
              You promise:

"Before they call, I will answer,
    while they are yet speaking, I will hear." (Isa 65:24)

In assurance we tell truth before you,
    As you hear our truth we may come again to praise and thanks,
        we may soon, not yet, not quickly,
        so listen, we bid, to so much not said until now
        Listen you great *Ear* of our future. Amen.

            June 20, 2002 (Montreat)

Dreaming with Freedom midst Chaos

Acts 2:1-21; John 14:8-17 / Pentecost

Ordinarily when things seem strange, we gather around the Gospel that is familiar and reliable. When things seem too new and threatening, we appeal to God who is old and established. When everything changes, we sing about the changeless God:

> Change and decay all around I see,
> O Thou who changest not, abide with me.

Ordinarily . . . except that Pentecost is not an ordinary time.

The difference is that it is God's own Spirit that causes the strangeness. It is God's Holy Spirit that is new among us. It is the Spirit of Jesus among us who changes everything. We speak this day of the Spirit, the church's feeble attempt to talk about the dangerous energy and presence of Jesus who is still alive in the world today. This Pentecost text tells about a moment in our faith, fifty days after Easter when Jesus had already ascended to power, and now the reign of Jesus sweeps into the church and makes all things new.

You can tell in the narrative that the coming of the Spirit with tongues like fire and with new speech scared people. And when people are scared, they try to explain it all in more familiar categories as a way of taming the event; so they judge the event to be one of drunkenness. That makes it familiar and therefore safer. Such an explanation of God's sweeping strangeness and newness, however, will not accommodate itself to our safe explanations. And so Peter, the voice of the church, bears witness to the event that falls outside conventional explanation. And we are children of that intrusion of God's liveliness that we remember and for which we hope.

I

Peter himself does not know what to say of this odd coming of God's future. Wisely, he quotes the Old Testament, because the Old Testament text illuminates what they are seeing. He quotes from the prophet Joel which itself is as odd as Pentecost. Nobody knows much about the book of Joel, but the synagogue had kept it for just such a moment as this. Joel had said in exotic, outrageous poetry:

> There will be portents in the heavens above
>   and signs on earth beneath,
>   blood, fire, and smoky mist.
> The sun will be turned to darkness
>   and the moon to blood,
>   before the coming of the Lord's great and glorious day.
>   (Acts 2:19-20; see Joel 2:30)

As you know, this poetry has lent itself to lots of weirdness. But remember, it is poetry, an attempt to state in hyperbolic images that the whole known world is under threat. That it will be worse before it gets better; lots worse.

Just the right poetry for us. Because it is among us worse and getting worse. Only a poet would talk about moons turning to blood, but we all notice the deep violence and brutality. Only a poet could speak of the sun turning to darkness, but we can see bewilderment and greed, and while we have not yet assaulted the sun, not yet, we can see the environment diminished and the ecosystem put deeply at risk. The poet wants to say, it is a dangerous time when all known life is put at deep risk.

That's how it is among us, a time of displacement and anxiety, all things strange, many things dangerous, all things beyond usual categories that require extreme speech, vivid usage beyond the familiar. That is how Joel got it said and why Peter quotes Joel.

II

How do we respond to bloody moons and dark suns and brutality and greed, and fear and poetry? Well we might try escape:

- we might try denial and pretend it is not so;
- we might try privatism and imagine we can have a private space of safety, an oasis of escape;
- we might try nostalgia, go backward and try to recover what was and is now gone.

But Peter knows that midst the bloody moons of fear and the dark suns of despair, another response has been made possible by the gift of God's sweeping Spirit. Again, he quotes the prophet Joel in order to get it said:

> God declares,
> that I will pour out my Spirit upon all flesh,
>> and your sons and your daughters shall prophesy,
> and your young men shall see visions,
>> and your old men shall dream dreams.
> Even upon my slaves, both men and women,
>> in those days I will pour out my Spirit; and they
>> shall prophesy. (Acts 2:17-18; see Joel 2:28-29)

What a mouthful! The Spirit of *freedom* and *courage* and *truth* will not drive people to *denial* or *privatism* or *nostalgia*. The ones upon whom God's Spirit comes will arise in the midst of bloody moons and dark suns and will utter a new future. They will stand in the midst of the failure and devastation and they will see visions and dream dreams and prophesy. They all will, old and young, men and women, slave and free, they all will, they will all be in the midst of the chaos. But they will not give in to the chaos. They will not let the despair define them. They will not surrender to fear or bewilderment or hate or brutality or greed or selfishness. None of them! Because they have something else more important on which to focus.

Peter, quoting Joel, imagines a community of free, bold, hope-filled men and women, boys and girls who stand in the very midst of the confusion that will be worse before it gets better, and who entertain God's future that will be given through and just past the bloody moons and the dark suns.

Pentecost is not just about a babble in the midst of confusion. Pentecost is about a liberated future that God has promised and that God will give. The same God who causes strangeness in the past is the God who gives newness in the future.

What a stunning vocation for the church, to stand free and hope-filled in a world gone fearful . . . and to think, imagine, dream, vision a future that God will yet enact. What a work of visioning for the church when society all around is paralyzed in fear, preoccupied by commodity, mesmerized by wealth, seeking endless power, and deeply, deeply frightened.

And here is this little community of visited people, not greedy, not fearful, not in despair,

- dreaming about the way of peace among peoples;
- visioning about justice between haves and have-nots;
- prophesying about an ordered earth, of greed curbed enough to respect the needs of the environment;
- not defensive about the others, but able to be inclusive of those not like us.

This community has no doubt that God's good world to come is not in the past, it is not in heaven, but it is on the earth, beyond bloody fear and scary chaos. What a place for the church to be on Pentecost!

III

Thus Peter had said two things by quoting Joel:

- it will get worse before it gets better;
- dream and vision in hope of God's new world.

And they responded to Peter, "What shall we do?" (v. 37). They understood that Peter (and Joel) are not for entertainment or dazzling or for mere thought. They understood immediately that they had to act. And we are told "they repented." They moved out beyond fear and paralysis and bewilderment. They were baptized, that is, they had their bodies marked by these new visitations of God. Think of baptism as the concrete physical outcome of Pentecost:

- these bodies marked in the midst of dark, bloody chaos;
- these bodies marked as carriers of God's future;
- these bodies marked to act differently, unafraid.

And, we are told, they took up new disciplines in order to enact their new identity of baptism:

- teaching of the apostles, truth already given;
- fellowship, being with other bodies marked by the Spirit;
- bread, pay attention to what you eat and with whom you eat;
- prayers, communion with the Holy One beyond themselves.

Pentecost may be flamboyant and dramatic. But it was enacted by the Spirit upon a receptive group of disciples who took their place in the body of disciplined believers. The text moves from the exotic to the daily, from imagery to disciplines. Who would have thought,

- that apostles' teaching is a match for a bloody moon?
- that table fellowship is answer to a dark sun?
- that daily bread is a powerful response to blood, fire, and smoky mist?

But it is! Pentecost moves beyond the exotic to a liberating, futuring community that is on the loose in the midst of the world's fear, despair, and disability. The book of Acts is the narrative enactment of Pentecosted people, those who bodily enact the future in the present tense in the public sphere. That is what the church has always done. That is what the church is doing now, free, unafraid, without despair:

> bodily in a way that confounds the authorities,
> futuring in a way that defies present strictures.

The people witnessing this strange community looked at this bodily futuring church and concluded that they were drunk? Well, yes, intoxicated with God's wind. The world is sober in its fear and its despair. But the community vented by the Spirit refuses such sobriety.

The book of Acts and the entire church tradition makes clear,

- the future of the world is in the hands of this little community unafraid of dark suns and bloody moons;
- this little community unafraid senses the good future of God and lives it now;
- this little community has such freedom because of disciplines that make it odd and free.

What a match—a little community of faith and the Spirit that surprises the world—held together by this hyperbolic poetry brought down to baptism and prayer and obedience and dreams.

> Fifty days after Easter,
> and many more days of intoxication yet to come!

Cathedral of St. Peter, Hamilton, New Zealand / June 3, 2001

On Reading Exodus 1–15

Our mothers and fathers groaned
> very loudly
> without restraint, in deep hurt.

> They groaned and since then many members of
>> our family have groaned over time
>> with hurt and need
>> with fear and violence,
>> with anger and despair,
>> with poverty and abuse.

> They groaned deep and loud . . .
>> just groaned . . .

And then we learned—utterly surprised—
> that that loud sound of groan came to you.
>> It was not addressed to you
>>> but it came to you.
>> It came to you, because you listen and pay attention,
>>> you are like a magnet for need,
>>> you draw hurt,
>>> you elicit groans.

And then . . . completely outside our categories . . .
>> you moved and acted and cared and intervened.
>> You saved and freed and liberated and rescued
>>> our mothers and fathers.
>> Our mothers and fathers then had no choice
>>> but to sing and dance
>>> to shake and rattle

in surprise
in delight
in *shalom,*
Shalom that you give as the world comes new.

This day . . . hear the new groans of many sisters and brothers,
hear and move and make new.

By twilight give us freedom to dance yet again,
to dance in joy and elation
that the world has become your domain
and we your glad servants
we your steady witnesses,
we your willing subjects.

We pray in the name of the carrier of our groans
and the doer of our miracles, even Jesus. Amen.

September 20, 2002

Joined in Suffering . . . Reliant on God's Power

Lamentations 1:1-6; 3:19-26; Luke 17:5-10; 2 Timothy 1:1-14

World Communion Sunday; 27th Sunday of Ordinary Time

Christians just now have peculiar work to do, and that is what we celebrate on World Communion Sunday; we have the whole world on our horizon in this hour of communion. In the Epistle reading, Paul writes to Timothy:

Join with me in suffering for the Gospel, relying on the power of God (Lam 1:8). Paul states the central mystery of our faith, *suffering power*, that is enacted in the death and resurrection of Jesus, and that is to be replicated in the life of the church. So my theme is that strange connection of suffering and power.

I

Have you ever heard a sermon on the book of Lamentations? Probably not, though it is the assigned Old Testament reading for today. The book of Lamentations is just that, a lament, five long poems of sadness, grief over the ancient city of Jerusalem that was destroyed by the Babylonians in 587 B.C.E. The Jews cried over that destruction, because the holy city was the focus of all their dreams and hopes, the sign of God's presence and fidelity to them, the gathering of all things precious and treasured. And then it was gone, gone by Babylonian invasion, but they said, gone by the anger of God . . . in any case gone!

And they wept. They wept for loss. They wept for abandonment. They wept in their deep hurt and despair. And the book of Lamentations lingers in the Bible, because Jews have never finished weeping over that loss that showed up again in the Nazi holocaust, and that likely is still at work in the present Israeli government with its fear and anxiety and brutality.

Christians have never much used and never much needed the book of Lamentations. Never needed and never used, because Christians have forever been triumphant and dominant, partly confident that Jesus is the winner, and partly privileged culturally, politically, and economically. As a result, our losses were never so deep . . . and no one did a "Final Solution" on us as on the Jews. We never used and never needed Lamentations, until we considered the cross and the crucifixion and the suffering love of Jesus and his call to enter the places of hurt with him.

So now, as we ponder lost Jerusalem and crucified Jesus and God's suffering love, as we hear Paul tell Timothy, "Join me in suffering for the Gospel," listen again to these old, deep cadences of loss, grief, and pain:

> How lonely sits the city
> > that once was full of people!
> How like a widow she has become,
> > she that was great among the nations!
> She that was a princess among the provinces
> > has become a vassal.
>
> She weeps bitterly in the night,
> > with tears on her cheeks;
> among all her lovers
> > she has no one to comfort her;
> all her friends have dealt treacherously with her,
> > they have become her enemies.
>
> Judah has gone into exile with suffering
> > and hard servitude;
> she lives now among the nations,
> > and finds no resting place;
> her pursuers have all overtaken her
> > in the midst of her distress.
>
> The roads to Zion mourn,
> > for no one comes to the festivals;
> all her gates are desolate,
> > her priests groan;
> her young girls grieve,
> > and her lot is bitter.
>
> Her foes have become the masters,
> > her enemies prosper,
> because the LORD has made her suffer

for the multitude of her transgressions;
her children have gone away,
    captives before the foe.

From daughter Zion has departed
    all her majesty.
Her princes have come like stags
    that find no pasture;
they fled without strength
    before the pursuer. (Lam 1:1-6)

It did not used to be so sad in Jerusalem. The city was full of people, great among the nations, a princess among the princes of the world. Did not used to be but now, lonely, like a widow, a vassal . . . humiliated, vulnerable, exposed, brutalized. It is a city imagined like an abused woman:

She weeps bitterly, tears on her cheeks,
none to comfort . . .

None to comfort, grief, loss, hurt, too deep to utter.

There is a reason that we now have the assigned text of Lamentations that we have not needed or used before. The reason is that, like those old Jews who saw Jerusalem devastated, we are watching the old world we have trusted and counted on vanish before our eyes. We are witnessing the demise of patterns of power and patterns of meaning that have seemed eternal. We are watching male privilege under threat, and white privilege is at risk. Western domination is now resisted, and I do not even need to observe that the old heterosexual assumptions are in doubt . . . old patterns of family and sexuality and medicine and education and justice . . . and anything else you might name, all now in jeopardy. There is a deep loss among us that gives way to deep anxiety that produces deep resentment and in many quarters brutality.

The big losses so public and seemingly cosmic spin off into immediate, local losses in the neighborhood. The index of violence and fear issues in public rage and more weapons and more prisons, state executions and more homelessness; and the outcome, midst our wealth and prosperity, is a kind of fearful hollowness at the center, midst privilege much less joy than we had anticipated.

Paul writes to Timothy:

Join me in suffering for the gospel.

And the poetry of Lamentations in deep need says wistfully,

> Is it nothing to you, all you who pass by?
>> Look and see
> if there is any sorrow like my sorrow,
>> which was brought upon me . . . (Lam 1:12)

Do you see? Do you notice? Do you care?

And here we are on World Communion Sunday. The good gifts of God, bread and wine as signs of presence and generosity, are spread before us. Also spread before us are the suffering of the world, the grief of loss, the steel edge of violence, the restless anxiety of need and rage, all around, distant, very close. We Christians notice both, signs of God's generous presence and signs of deep need . . . notice both and embrace both, because in our faith they come together.

The world does not notice, did not notice Jerusalem in crisis, does not notice wretchedness and violence and poverty alongside our ease. But because we are so close to Jesus, we notice and engage. Suffering in the Gospel is not masochistic or Lenten self-denial. It is, rather, acting and living and praying and sharing in the awareness that our life is as one with those who suffer. And when we notice as Jesus notices, we find ourselves transformed,

> away from self-sufficiency to solidarity,
> away from private privilege to communal engagement,
> away from hard, dismissive indifference to compassion.

Paul's invitation to join in suffering is not a bid for a specific act. It is rather an invitation to a different form of life, a different presence in the world, a mode of life that participates in the healing of the world.

II

Now it may occur to you, as it has to me, that if we notice and care fully, if we cry with the hurting, stand in compassion with the broken, and share with the hollow, will we not be devoured by the grief, devoured by grief while the uncaring world goes its buoyant way without bothering? It is an old temptation among us to think so much about the need of the world that we get bogged down in our own depression, for the losses are too deep and the needs are too great for our capacity.

But Paul already knows about this problem. And so he writes to Timothy:

> Join me in suffering for the gospel . . . relying upon the power of God, who saved us and called us with a holy calling, not according to our works but according to his own purpose and grace. (vv. 8-9)

The antidote to depression is our calling in God's purpose. The ground for well-being midst suffering is the power of God. We gather on this communion Sunday to testify to each other that the suffering of the world all around us is in the midst of God's power from which we act freely in caring ways of solidarity.

Of course the power of God seems thin and flimsy in the face of loss and brutality and anxiety and hollowness. But Christians from the beginning have known and have staked their lives on the conviction that God's gift of faith to us and God's call for us to be different in the world are supported by God's power that we have seen in the resurrection of Jesus and that we know will prevail in the world in God's good time.

The poetry in Lamentations asserts the same conviction of faith in God. In looking straight into the loss of Jerusalem, the poet says:

> My soul is bereft of peace;
>> I have forgotten what happiness is;
> so I say, "Gone is my glory,
>> and all that I had hoped for from the LORD." (Lam 3:17-18)

The sense of loss, hurt, and abandonment is so great that it drowns out any hope.

But then, three verses later, the poet has a new voice:

> This I call to mind,
>> and therefore I have hope. (v. 21)

It is by remembering God's power in past times that one can be engaged in suffering in present time. This is what the poet remembers:

> The steadfast love of the LORD never ceases,
>> his mercies never come to an end;
> they are new every morning;
>> great is your faithfulness. (vv. 22-23)

Here are the three great words in the Old Testament bespeaking the power of God: *steadfast love, mercy, faithfulness*. Israel finds God to be utterly reliable midst any and every loss. The church has found God to be utterly reliable midst every suffering. Even now as we speak, all around the world there are believers who know God's steadfast love, mercy, and faithfulness that are reliable midst every need. So Paul writes to Timothy, " . . . relying on God's power." For the power of God is reliable!

It is people who do not trust God's faithfulness, who do not know God's mercy and who have no sense of God's faithfulness, who engage in denial and cannot face the loss going on all around us. It is the loss of that memory that lets people fall into anxiety, resentfulness, and destructiveness.

But we, as Christians, we baptized Christians who eat broken bread and drink poured out wine, we are different. We know about God's reliable power—steadfast love, mercy, faithfulness—and so we do not flinch from the suffering of the world. We come to it with freedom and confidence, knowing that God entrusts to us the capacity to heal and transform. And so to the table,

> there spread before us are all the hurts and losses of the world,
> there spread before us is the power of God, given as steadfast
> love, mercy, and faithfulness.

We have not "a spirit of cowardice, but of a spirit of power and of love and of self-discipline" (1 Tim 1:7). We really are different! We are unafraid, with peculiar work to do!

Westminster Presbyterian Church, Durham, North Carolina / October 7, 2001
during the beginning of the U.S. military action in Afghanistan

On Beginning Lament Psalms

You are the God from whom no secret can be hid.

You are the God of truth
    to whom the truth must be told.

And so we bring to you
    the truth of the world:
        the truth of hunger and poverty,
        the truth of need and abandonment and anxiety,
        the truth of hurt and dying,
        the truth of violence and war.

All these truths we submit to your more
    powerful life-giving truth.

So we bid you, truth-doing God,
    veto the hunger and poverty in our world,
    override the need and abandonment and anxiety
        so palpable among us,
    cancel out the hurt and the dying
        so pervasive in our world,
    move peaceably against violence
        and enact your *shalom*
            in the face of our threats of war.

We do not hold back from you
    the truth of our need.

Do not hold back from us
     the gospel truth of your mercy
                              compassion and
                              forgiveness.

Sway us from our deep distortion
     into your deep goodness
     that we and our world may again,
              by your verdict,
              be "Very good." Amen.

September 19, 2002

Missing by Nine Miles

Isaiah 60:1-7; Matthew 2:1-12 / Epiphany

Everybody knows about the three wise men coming to the Christ child. No surprise there. Everybody knows about them bringing "gold, and frankincense, and myrrh," and singing "We Three Kings of Orient Are." No surprise there. No surprise, unless you pay close attention to the way in which Matthew tells the story. But that will require you to listen very carefully. Because behind the single visit of the Eastern intellectuals passing through Jerusalem enroute to Bethlehem, there are some very tricky things going on in the text of Matthew.

I

This notion of rich, wise guys from the East coming to Jerusalem did not happen for the first time in Matthew. Matthew is not the first one who imagined how that vision might turn out. What you need to know is that Matthew got the story line and plot from Isaiah 60, which we read this morning. What you need to know is that Isaiah 60 is a very old poem recited to Jews in Jerusalem about 580 B.C.E. These Jews had been sent away from Jerusalem in exile in Iraq for a couple generations. They came back to the bombed-out city of Jerusalem, and they found it in shambles without a viable economy and without much ground for new possibility. They were disappointed and ready to despair, for who wants to live in a city where the towers are torn down and the economy has failed and nobody can think what to do about it?

In the middle of that mess in Jerusalem about 580 B.C.E., there was this amazing poet who invited his depressed, discouraged contemporaries to look up and hope and expect newness in the city that God would give again. He promised that everything would change in Jerusalem because God is about to do good:

> Arise, shine; for your light has come . . .
> the LORD will arise upon you,
>   and his glory will appear over you. (Isa 60:1-2)

The poet anticipates that Jerusalem would become a beehive of productivity and prosperity, the new center of international trade. The nations, their leaders and traders, would come, and Jerusalem would consequently prosper:

> Nations shall come to your light,
>   and kings to the brightness of your dawn . . .
> the wealth of the nations shall come to you. (vv. 3, 5)

Specifically the poet imagined that there would be great camel caravans that would come from Asia loaded with commercial goods that would cause prosperity in the beloved city:

> A multitude of camels shall cover you,
> [that's where we get the "three orientals" on camels]
>   the young camels of Midian and Ephah. (v. 6a)

More specifically, they will bring exotic goods, especially rare spices:

> They shall bring gold and frankincense,
>   and shall proclaim the praise of the LORD. (v. 6b)

This is a great cause for celebration, because God, in this poem, has promised to make the city of Jerusalem work effectively in peace and prosperity. The poem contradicts the present dysfunction of the city. This is a promise from God, thus very sure.

Matthew is a retelling of that old poem. The wise men, like Matthew, had read and knew about Isaiah 60. As a result, they knew they were to come to Jerusalem. They knew they were to bring rare spices, gold and frankincense and myrrh. They knew, most importantly, that they would there find the new king of all peace and prosperity. So that Matthew says:

> Wise men came from the East to Jerusalem asking,
> "Where is the child who has been born king of the Jews?"
> (Matt 2:2)

They had pondered Isaiah 60 and knew what was promised. But then we are told:

> When Herod [the current king in Jerusalem] heard them,
> he was frightened, and all Jerusalem with him. (v. 3)

They were frightened because a new king in Jerusalem would be a threat to the old king and to the old order. All those who trusted in and benefited from the old order were deeply upset at the prospect of newness.

II

And then a very strange thing happened. In his panic, we are told, Herod arranged a consultation with the leading Old Testament scholars in his society, and said to them, "Tell me about Isaiah 60. What is all this business about these camels and gold and frankincense and myrrh right out my window?"

The scholars took some time to study up and prepare a report fit for a king. They came back to Herod and they reported: You have got the wrong text. And the wise men outside your window have attended to the wrong text as a basis for their travel. When you have the wrong text, you will get everything wrong. The text you (Herod and the wise men) have been reading from Isaiah 60 will mislead you . . . because that text suggests that Jerusalem will prosper and have great urban wealth and will be restored as the center of the global economy; in that scenario, the urban elites can recover their former power and prestige, and everything will be like normal . . . only more so. Nothing will have to change!

Well, Herod did not like that verdict from his tenured advisors. So he said defiantly to his scholar-advisors, "Well, do you have a better text?" The scholars were indeed frightened of the mad king; even though they had tenure they were not safe. But they told him, with some trepidation, "My Lord, we think the right text is not Isaiah 60; rather it is Micah 5:2-4, which is as follows":

> But you, O Bethlehem of Ephrathah,
>   who are one of the little clans of Judah,
> from you shall come forth for me
>   one who is to rule in Israel,

whose origin is from of old,
from ancient days . . . .
And he shall stand and feed his flock in the strength of
the LORD,
in the majesty of the name of the LORD his God.
And they shall live secure, for now he shall be great
to the ends of the earth;
and he shall be the one of peace.

That text, from the lips of the rural peasant Micah, is the voice of a peasant hope for the future. It is not impressed with high towers and great arenas, banks and great urban achievements. The little ones think rather about a different future, as yet unaccomplished, in a peasant land that will be organized for well-being in resistance to the great imperial threat. It anticipates a common leader who will bring well-being to his people, not by great political ambition, but by attentiveness to the facts of folk on the ground. This is what they told Herod, at great risk to their careers, as well as to their safety.

As a result, Herod had to go back and tell the Eastern intellectuals the truth that must have steamed them, too, the truth that must have made the Jerusalem king choke with anger and fear. He told them . . . and the rest is history. They headed for the little town of Bethlehem, the hometown of King David, the birthplace of Jesus, a little rural place, dusty, unnoticed, unpretentious Bethlehem named by Micah. The place had not yet become a great tourist attraction, or a place of contest between occupying armies. The village was quite beside the point for the great imperial ambitions of "peace and prosperity." This was the proper milieu for this unnoticed, uncelebrated peasant birth of the one who was to offer a deep alternative to the arrogant learning of the intellectuals and the arrogant power of great urban might . . . this new presence from Bethlehem who would confound kings and intellectuals and who would evoke the savage violence of Herod. It is no wonder that the Eastern intellectuals, smitten by this new mode of foolishness that is wiser than human wisdom, went home by an alternative route.

III

This narrative of Epiphany is a story of *two texts*. *Isaiah 60* offers a dream of urban power and prosperity; *Micah 2* gives its promise of an alternative future that is modest but confident. The narrative of epiphany is the story of *two human communities*: *Jerusalem* with its great pretensions about the future and the little peasant village of *Bethlehem* with its modest promises known only by the poet. This narrative of epiphany is an announcement of *two ways of living* between which we are always choosing, a way that is a quick *"return to normalcy"* in a triumphalist mode and a way that *dreams of an alternative* that comes in innocence and in a hope that confounds all our usual pretensions.

This second text is not a text to idealize rural life at the expense of urban life. It is rather an invitation to receive life given in vulnerability rather than a life of self-sufficiency that contains within it its own seeds of destruction. It is no wonder that Herod was flabbergasted and enraged at the conclusions of his advisors; he took steps to crush the threat of the new alternative in order to protect the way it used to be. It is amazing—the true accent of epiphany—that the wise men did not resist the alternative and went on to the village. Rather than hesitate or resist, with great courage they reorganized their great wealth and their great learning, reorienting themselves and their impressive lives around this Little One who is uncredentialed but who becomes God's way of newness in the world.

If you know anything about the geography of the "Holy Land," you know that Bethlehem is nine miles south of Jerusalem. Or better to say Jerusalem is nine miles north of Bethlehem. The wise men had a long intellectual history of erudition and a long-term practice of mastery. But they had missed their goal by nine miles. They miscalculated by that much. Herod thought he was in the epicenter of God's future; but he had miscalculated as well by nine miles. This is a very long nine miles, long and demanding, long for the Eastern intellectuals. It was far too long and too demanding for Herod who would rather hold on to his rage, wave his patriotic flag, and defend the way it used to be, before the intrusion from nine miles off center.

It is mind-boggling to think how the story might have gone, had Herod's interpreters not remembered Micah 2 and just told the story according to the high successes of Isaiah 60. They would have mistakenly thought that the future belongs to power, prestige, and control. I suggest that the task among us is to let *the vulnerability of Micah 2* disrupt *the self-congratulations of Isaiah 60*. Or to put it differently, the great work of Epiphany is to recognize that most of us are looking for what God promises in the wrong place, wrong by nine miles. The invitation issued among us is to travel those nine hard, demanding miles to vulnerability and away from self-sufficiency. Epiphany is, moreover, a good time to take that hard, unwelcome journey, for September 11 still reminds about the shambles that can come through our excessive pretension. The way beyond the shambles, this text from Micah suggests, is not about glory and remembered security and past prosperity. The way of the Christ child, echoing Micah, is

> vulnerability,
> neighborliness,
> generosity,

a modest future with spears into pruning hooks and swords into plowshares. As Micah said in another place, "not learning war anymore" (4:3).

This is an alternative to ponder, a hard, slow nine miles. The wise men, the eager nations ready for an alternative, made the trip all nine miles. It would be ironic among us if the "outsiders" made that move and we who are God's own people resisted. Imagine a nine-mile trip . . . and a very different way home!

Plymouth Congregational Church (UCC), Coconut Grove, Florida / January 6, 2002

On Reading Samuel

We confess you to be King and Shepherd of our lives,
               Ruler of Public Power,
               Mother in Israel.

We watch the endless shenanigans
        of power:
                of corruption
                of greed
                of self-indulgence
                of violence.

And we are aware that you call and choose
        human agents to manage public power.
      Such human agents . . . so wise and/or stupid
                so brave and/or worldly
                so pure and/or corrupt.

      You call little ones like David,
      You call those without credentials . . .
                like Jesus.
      You call such governors as Roy,
           such presidents as George,
           such chairmen as Arafat.

      You call and work your purposes . . .
           in and through and in spite of . . .

You rule—and we wish it were more like a church camp—but it is not!
      We are sobered to your will and to our task. Amen.

On Reading Samuel / October 1, 2002

The Big Yes

Exodus 17:1-7; Psalm 95; John 4:5-15 [16–42] / Third Sunday in Lent

O ur Old Testament story puts Israel in the wilderness between slavery and the land of promise. Israel has a rich and embarrassing memory of the wilderness, about how Israel conducted itself in a time of danger and deficit. The theme of wilderness is an appropriate one for Lent, for Lent is about being in thin places without resources and being driven back to the elemental reality of God, the reliability of God, and our capacity to trust God in the thin places where there are no other resources. The theme of wilderness—by way of Lent—is a useful one for us now. Indeed, the context of the U.S.—in our long season of fear, anxiety, and violence—is being driven back to wilderness questions about the reality of God, the reliability of God, and our capacity to trust God in the thin places where there are no other resources for life.

I

The scene is at Rephidim in the wilderness. Nobody knows where that was. It is simply a place with a lack. It was a dry, hot place, and they had no water. Imagine, no water, the most elemental requirement for life, the scarcest commodity in the wilderness, and they had none. They could not produce any for themselves. There were no wells. They had no adequate substitutes for water that could possibly sustain them. The focus is upon their deep need and upon the way in which the deepest question of faith is connected to the deepest material reality of life. (Likely you know that even now the scarcity of water is an acute one around the world, so that it is quipped, "The next great war will not be about *oil* but about *water*.") So they complained, thinking they were entitled to water. They argued with Moses who was supposed to assure the water supply. Finally they must come face-to-face with God, because they have no alternative. That is what Lent is about, is it not? . . . to come face-to-face with God in need because there is no alternative. Lent is not about guilt or even about repentance or giving up some convenient extra. It is rather about the raw, deepest need in our life.

What happens in this transaction is that the *water question* (material, concrete support for life) is turned into *the God Question* concerning the one who "leads us beside still waters . . . " As a result they dared to ask the question, "Is the Lord among us or not?" The Bible does not everywhere assume that God is present, but knows about the dry places where God's absence is overwhelming. They asked *the God question* about *the water problem,* because they knew they were up against it in their need and had no alterative. The Israelites, in their quarrelsome challenge, articulated the song of Eliza Doolittle to Freddie in "My Fair Lady," "Don't talk of love, show me!" "Don't talk of water, show me." Don't give me theological formulations, do something concrete. This is a demanding, quarrelsome engagement, but the Israelites in their anxiety were exceedingly practical. They did not want a God who would not deliver on the real stuff needed to make life possible.

II

And then quite tersely, God, with an assist from Moses, answers the anxiety of Israel:

> Go on ahead of the people, and take some of the elders of Israel with you; take in your hand the staff with which you struck the Nile, and go. I will be standing there in front of you on the rock of Horeb. Strike the rock, and water will come out of it, so that the people may drink. (vv. 5-6)

God hears the cries of Israel. God answers decisively. God gives water. God gives the water of life. And when God gives water for life, Israel's deep question is answered: Yes: The Lord is among us! Yes, God has the capacity to transpose wilderness into an arena for life. Yes, God is reliable. Yes, God is faithful. Yes, God is an adequate source for life in a context of scarcity and anxiety. This is the "Big Yes" of God, the one about whom Paul writes:

> As surely as God is faithful, our word to you has not been "Yes and No." For the Son of God, Jesus Christ, whom we

proclaimed among you, Silvanus and Timothy and I, was not "Yes and No"; but in him it is always "Yes." For in him every one of God's promises is a "Yes." For this reason it is through him that we say the "Amen," to the glory of God. (2 Cor 1:18-20)

"Always Yes!" Israel can remember not only that water was given by God, but remembers how it was given. Like blood from a turnip, like a purse from the ear of a sow, water from rock, food from hunger, life from death, joy from sorrow, Yes from No, well-being from anxiety. The story does not explain, any more than we explain Easter after Friday, well-being after Lent. And the reason we do not explain is that we are looking to God, the one who holds all circumstances and all emergencies, all possibilities and all needs and all gifts in God's own hand, the one who says "yes." The story is about God's inexplicable capacity to do well-being in a world that has been shut down. *Yes* even in wilderness, *yes* in Lent, *yes* from rock, *yes* to thirst. *Yes* to us, *yes* to the world, the story is about being dazzled beyond every explanation, *Yes, Yes, Yes!*

III

Israel did not quit on the story with its good news. So we carry it in three directions after the resounding Yes of the water-giving, rock-slapping, life-sustaining Yes of God. Listen for all three:

1. While the narrative memory of Exodus 17 is about the miraculous Yes of God to give water in the desert, the event is also remembered negatively as a time when Israel did not in fact trust God, but tested God by requiring God to meet a concrete, material criterion. That is, trust would have known, without anxiety or anger, that God would have provided what was needed; but distrust is the reduction of God to material exhibit. This negative judgment about the story is given in Psalm 95. I don't know what you noticed as we heard Psalm 95. The first part of the Psalm is lovely as well as familiar to us. It is a glad celebrative entry into God's presence:

O come, let us sing to the LORD;
    let us make a joyful noise to the rock of our salvation!
Let us come into his presence with thanksgiving;
    let us make a joyful noise to him with songs of praise! . . .

O come, let us worship and bow down,
　　let us kneel before the LORD, our Maker! (vv. 1-2, 6)

This is followed by great affirmations about God's great power as creator:

For the LORD is a great God,
　　and a great King above all gods,
In his hand are the depths of the earth;
　　the heights of the mountains are his also.
The sea is his, for he made it,
　　and the dry land, which his hands have formed. (vv. 3-5)

And there is a ready acceptance of identity as God's people:

For he is our God,
　　and we are the people of his pasture,
　　and the sheep of his hand. (v. 7a)

Well, they should have left it there and all would be well. But the psalm does not end there. The text goes on to assert:

- that they did not trust God as creator to give water;
- that they did not accept identity as God's cared-for people.

And so the rest of the psalm turns negative, the part of the psalm we mostly avoid:

O that today you would listen to his voice!
　　Do not harden your hearts, as at Meribah,
　　as on the day at Massah in the wilderness,
when your ancestors tested me,
　　and put me to the proof...
For forty years I loathed that generation ...
Therefore in my anger I swore,
"They shall not enter my rest." (vv. 7b-11)

God does not like to be tested. God does not want to jump through our hoops, because God will give what is needed without coercive demands. The narrative is one of not trusting God and making material gifts the measure of God's godness.

2. Our text is taken up in an act of imagination in the narrative of John 4, our Gospel reading. In this narrative, the beginning point is that Jesus asks for water from a woman. But then Jesus quickly reverses field, to say to the woman, I ask you for water, but you should have asked me for water, because I am the real source of water. And then Jesus says to her:

> Everyone who drinks of this water will be thirsty again, but those who drink of the water that I will give them will never be thirsty. The water that I will give will become in them a spring of water gushing up to eternal life. (John 4:13-14)

And the woman, in trust, responds:

> Sir, give me this water, so that I may never be thirsty or have to keep coming here to draw water. (v. 15)

The exchange is a dramatic way to make the claim that in this story, Jesus is doing what only God can do, that is, Jesus is the exhibit of the life-giving power of God. It is only God—and so Jesus—who gives water in a barren land. It is only God—and so Jesus—who can turn our wilderness into livable land. It is only God—and so Jesus—who can turn the reality of death into the stunning gift of life.

It is clear that the gospel narrative has taken the concrete-material reality of water and transposed it into a metaphor. Water is now gospel; water is the good news. Water is sign and symbol that in Jesus we are given a new quality of life, as the text says, "a spring of water gushing up to eternal life." This is extraordinary good news that in the life of this defeated woman, durable quenching is possible. It was outrageous good news that from the hard rock of a failed life durable quenching happens, good news for ancient Israel in the wilderness, good news for the woman thirsting for a better life, good news for us in a culture of paralyzing anxiety.

3. So the story moves:

- to show that doubting God's care is an act of rebellion when we are invited to trust;

- to show that Jesus is seen in the Gospel to be one who satisfies our deepest thirsts.

But let me add now a third extrapolation that concerns us in the midst of Lent in the U.S. Wilderness fits for us, a new awareness that we live in a world of resources that are thinner than we had imagined. I suspect that those of us who trust the Gospel are deeply torn, on the one hand committed to the truth of Jesus as the one who gives "water gushing up to eternal life." At the same time, however, so anxious and uncertain that we seek in many other places for water, not recognizing that the barren land of anxiety contains many mirages that look like remembered water, but are not really water that can quench.

In a different context the prophet Jeremiah accused the people of God:

> My people have committed two evils:
>> they have forsaken me,
> the fountain of living water,
>> and dug out cisterns for themselves,
> cracked cisterns
>> that can hold no water. (Jer 2:13)

The two sins of the people of God are (a) to forsake the true God of living water and (b) to dig out for ourselves cracked cisterns that can hold no water. We do the latter in our anxiety, seeking to secure our own water supply. The list of broken cisterns we have dug for ourselves is long and obvious. It may include our endless pursuit of more sex or bigger cars or larger portfolios or better weapons or whatever. It always comes down to the consumer goods of sex, money, power, and violence. Our society is deep into such mistaken self-security, a powerful temptation to us all.

Lent is a time to ponder the broken cisterns where we have tried to store our own water supply. Have you noticed that we stay thirsty? Have you noticed that we are not by such resources made happy—or safe—or satisfied? Lent is a time for noticing and choosing again, choosing what the world doubts:

- a rock in a hard place from which God brings water;
- a rabbi at a well with a promise never to thirst again.

And we with our deep thirst, unquenched, stand by the well with deep yearning:

> Sir: give me this water;
>   give me this water,
>   so that I may never again be thirsty
>   or have to keep coming here to draw water.

What a Lent: Give me this water and I will never thirst again!

Second Presbyterian Church, Roanoke, Virginia / March 3, 2002

On Reading the Sinai Pericope

Your mountain erupted and disturbed the landscape.
Your voice disrupted and took our breath away.
> You spoke—in your own voice.
> You addressed us, willing to engage.
> You said "Thou" and we were connected to you.
> You said "Thou shalt" and we were summoned.
> You said "Thou shalt not," and we were under discipline.
You gave us your dream and your hope
And we answered with a simple *yes*.
> Yes, we sign on with you.
> Yes, we will be your people.
> Yes, we will embrace your vision.
> Yes, we will follow your commands.
We are addressed, summoned, signed on as your people.
We live from your mouth in utterance.
We live back to you in gladness and expectation,
> sure enough—even on hard days—that in the midst of our
> obedience
>> Your rule will come finally among us.
We wait in eager longing and are glad for the good freedom
>> your commands give. Amen.

September 25, 2002

Saints Remembered and Saints to Come

Isaiah 43:16-21; Hebrews 11:8-16, 39-40

Mary and I are very glad to be at Peace Church for this wondrous celebration of 100 years. It is a first time for Mary to be in Tilden. As some of you will know, my father August was pastor here from 1931 to 1935. After we moved away to Kansas, I was here only one other time with my family for a brief visit in 1948. My father, who died in 1970, and my mother, who died in 1995, had happy memories of days in Tilden. Since I was only three when we moved away, my memories are only secondhand:

- the deep snows of which we have pictures that can still make one shiver;
- the deep depression that shaped my family and my way of thinking about money and about life;
- special times with the Sharpless family, and the fact that Lucille (Winder) was my babysitter.

And since I have grown up to be a confirmed St. Louis Cardinal baseball fan, I have always been glad to be from the same hometown as Richie Ashburn. That is about all I know, except that I root vigorously, regularly, for the Cornhuskers.

I

That is about all I know about Peace Church. But let me tell you what else I know. I know that in this place for 100 years, first in German and then in English, we have said together,

I believe in the Holy Spirit,
the holy catholic church
(or alternatively, "the one holy universal Christian church"),
and in the communion of saints.

We connected *spirit* and *church* and *saints*. On this anniversary, we affirm that the spirit has been in this church all this time,

> creating and renewing the church of Jesus Christ,
> binding in covenant faithful people of all ages, tongues, and races.

That is what we believe.

And we believe that the church in this place has been a gathering place for the saints of God, and that is my subject this morning. In our evangelical faith, we do not mean what popular religion has come to mean by saints; rather, we mean men and women, boys and girls, who love the Lord and who live lives that show it. To be sure, in this congregation, like every congregation, some have been not so saintly, and occasionally even the saints act in less than saintly ways. Nonetheless, by speaking of the communion of saints, we confess,

1. that our dead who have died in faith are safely with God,

2. that we who live in the church are deeply connected not only to our Lord, but to our loved ones who lived and died in the Lord. And so we can sing:

> Yet we on earth have union with God the three in one,
> and mystic sweet communion with those whose rest is won,
> O happy ones and holy, God give us grace that we,
> like them the meek and lowly may live eternally.

II

So my first theme concerns the saints of the past. I have collected three ways of speaking about saints:

1. In a church window where the sun shown through, a little girl said, "Oh yes, saints are the ones through whom the light comes upon us." And there have been saints in this church through whom the light has shown.

2. Saints are people who know the primal language of the "other," that is, who are kind and generous toward others and who respect people who are not like us. Others of different race and age and class and culture and ethnic community, and now we even say, other sexual orientation. Many of us fear the other, but saints know that the other may be where God meets us.

3. Saints are those who do not run and hide when they smell death. They are unafraid of suffering, and they stay present in love and mercy where there is dying and illness and violence.

So think of these three marks of the church:

- where the light comes;
- where others are valued, and
- where death smells and we stay.

And then think of Peace Church. All this time, it has been a place where the saints have gathered; many men and women, boys and girls, have gathered who have trusted God and have grown in faith and lived in discipleship. It is an awesome memory among us!

The text we read from Hebrews 11 must have been written for such an anniversary. It takes a longer vista of history than this congregation has, a very old history that reaches back in faith to the beginning in Abraham and Sarah, our first parents in faith, and it even goes behind them to remember Cain and Abel and Noah. It reaches that far back, but it will permit us to add at the other end and to bring the list of the faithful up-to-date by the names of our grandparents and parents and even our own names as key players in our hundred years that is a part of that longer memory.

What it says about this long list of remembered people is that every one of them lived by faith. Faith is the willingness to trust our lives and our future to God, even when God does not appear to be as reliable as other, more immediate supports. Faith is readiness to risk life on the promises of God without holding back. So the text affirms:

> By faith our ancestors received approval from God;
> God liked how they lived!
> By faith, we understand that worlds are prepared by the word
> of God;
> the world belongs to God;
> By faith, and not by sight,
> By faith and not by financial security,
> By faith and not by doctrinal certitude,
> By faith and not by popular culture,
> By faith and not by our morality.

That is how the church has lived; and the church will not live long or host the goodness and power of God unless there are a strong number of people who believe the good news of the Gospel and stake their lives on the very truth of God that the world thinks is foolishness. The text sets high expectations for the faithful and then says that over the centuries that is how the faithful have been, at their best entrusting their lives to God, not needing to be in control, not needing to see the outcomes, by faith and not by sight.

In our joy at this anniversary, this day is a sobering one for us, because we name and remember the gutsy, generous people before us who were determined that Jesus is the good news, who were convinced that God should be obeyed in this place, who were very sure that the good news of Jesus has to do not only with our personal lives but also with our public life and all the stark issues of race and economics and housing and schools, all those arenas over which Jesus Christ is Lord. The sturdy folk in this church have always trusted that Jesus is Lord in this town and in this world. If you think about it, it takes your breath away, that some have confessed that and lived it for one hundred years.

The text says about all those men and women and boys and girls of faith in this place and in every place like this place,

> They did not spend their time thinking of the land they had left behind, that they could go back to it. They did not spend their energy wishing for the good old days and engaging in nostalgia. But they desired a better country. Therefore God is not ashamed to be called their God.

The men and women of faith in this long recital did not look back but forward, so that the question of faith is only about what is next in the mission of God. All the faithful folk looked forward to risk, not backward to safety. And we remember them today and give thanks.

III

But as we remember we also look forward. The church in joy and gratitude and dazzlement for these hundred years must consciously, deliberately turn its face away from that glorious past and face the future where God always meets us. This anniversary text in Hebrews 11 goes on and on about the past. After Abraham and Sarah there are

Isaac and Jacob and Joseph and Moses and Gideon and Samson and Samuel and David and the prophets, all the people we learned about in Sunday school. The text talks about their suffering and faithfulness, their toughness and resilience, and then at the end, there are just two quick verses to finish the long chapter:

> Yet all these, though they were commended for their faith, did not receive what was promised, since God has provided something better so that they would not, apart from us, be made perfect. (vv. 39-40)

I believe the entire chapter was written in order to get to these two verses and second task of an anniversary. The ending of the chapter affirms that all these ancestors did well, but they did not get there. They did not receive the full promise. The kingdom of God did not come in their lifetime, and all the deep issues of God's mission in this city remain unfinished and unsettled. They did not get it all done. And then it says, you might think they were perfect people of faith. Truth to tell, they would not, apart from us, be made perfect.

It is a very strange statement: How *their lives* count depends on *our lives*. How well they did is determined by how well we do. What we do decides the quality of their faith. The present actions of the faithful decide about the significance of the past. This letter to the Hebrews is written to people in the early church when faith was risky and dangerous. The letter is written to say to the listening congregation, "Everything is up to you." You get to decide the value of what they did. Do you know about keeping score in bowling? When you bowl a frame, if you get a spare or a strike you mark it down; but what you bowl in the next frame or two determines the value of what you have already done in the previous frame. The intergenerational mystery of the church is like that. The value of the first hundred years in the eyes of God depends upon what is done now.

That gives today and tomorrow and the next decades and the next century of this church enormous power over the past. You now can determine what this history adds up to. It gives this present generation the capacity to invalidate a hundred years of faith by copping out. But it also gives this generation the immense opportunity to maximize and enhance what has been done here.

So consider, this church has contributed to many church programs and mission efforts, but how that counts *depends on now*.

Thus the second task of the church on an anniversary occasion is to begin asking what will the church be now, what now will we do in a church that lives in a community that has become ethnically complex in a world that is deep in bewilderment and violence, when old ways are fading? How deep now will it go to faith, how serious now about inviting the young into obedience, how to face now the life and death issues facing our society? Remember, these ancestors in faith desired a better country, and now we inherit the chance for a better faith, a better city, a better mission from God.

So this is a time at Peace Church to decide about the next hundred years and the communion of saints in time to come:

- Decide now to be the people in the future through whom the light of God comes;
- Decide now to be the people who value and respect others, the ones not like us;
- Decide now to be the people who stay and care when they smell death.

IV

The Old Testament text from Isaiah was written in a like situation to a community of faith in ancient Israel in a time of exile; they had to decide about a new future. Some were nostalgic and thought they could recover better days now gone. But this text blurts out the heavy truth to them and to us:

Do not remember former things.

What a thing to say on an anniversary!

Behold I am doing a new thing; can't you see it?

The new thing God was doing then was calling exiles to be a different kind of community. The new thing God was calling to the church was to be passionately faithful. The new thing God is doing in this church is putting it down in a bewildered society where haves and have-nots grow more tense with each other, where consumer values seduce us and reduce everything to wealth and security, where a new kind of pluralism brings all kinds of strange people into the community that used to be just for us. That's the new place for the church, and it is happening so quickly that we scarcely notice. What a glorious moment this is, that this church can now make decisions about its life and its faith and its mission and its budget and its worship, that will validate and maximize and enhance the past hundred years.

The Isaiah text promises that God,
> will make a highway in wilderness places,
> a path to the future,
> God will give water in desert places,
> God will give drink to my chosen people,
> wine and bread and sustenance,
> That they might declare my praise.

Think of another hundred years in this place of prayer and mission, of risk and joy, of obedience and trust, all the ways of living by faith, and this is the moment to remember and then to see God's newness happening all around us, springing up among us like an Easter gift. Old saints remembered in love, new saints emerging, faithful their whole lives through. That is why the hymn goes like this:

> I sing a song for the saints of God,
> faithful their whole lives through,
> who bravely labored, lived and died
> for the God they loved and knew.
> And one was a doctor and one was a queen,
> and another a shepherd in pastures green.
> They were saints of God, if you know what I mean,
> God help me to be one too.

Peace UCC in Tilden, Nebraska / April 7, 2002
on the occasion of the 100th anniversary of the preacher's home church

On Reading Psalm 3

You watcher of men,
You monitor of women,
You supervisor of boys and girls,
    You who watch and know and observe,
    You are the one from whom no secret can be hid.

You know when we sit down and when we rise up,
You know when we go out and when we come in,
You know our great trust in you
        and our gratitude toward you.

But you also know our anxiety before you,
      our need to hide,
      our readiness to deceive,
Yet you are "the one from whom no secret can be hid."

So we pray that we may be "full of truth"
      even as you are "full of grace and truth";
We pray for freedom to tell you the full truth of our life:
    Our hopes that are too large to imagine,
    Our fears that are too deep to manage,
    Our hates that are too hot to act upon,
    Our loneliness that is too heavy to bear,
    Our resentments that eat at us,
    Our doubts that you care or will care enough.

Make us *truth-tellers* that we may move beyond
      our endless circles of deception and self-
      deception . . .

plain enough to address you,
simple enough to "will one thing,"
honest enough to utter and move on having sounded ourselves
fully to you. Amen.

June 19, 2002 (Montreat)

The Secret of Survival

Jeremiah 20:7-13; Matthew 6:1-8

In chapter 19, Jeremiah declares that "this people" and "this city" arc like a broken pot that cannot be mended. When he announced this devastating verdict upon the Jerusalem establishment, he predictably evoked harsh response. In chapter 20, Pashur, a high sacral bureaucrat who in this chapter enjoys his fifteen minutes of fame, arrested Jeremiah as an enemy of the state. He punished him by putting him in stocks "in the Upper Benjamin Gate" of the temple. This caused Jeremiah in turn to unleash a strong invective against the official and against all Judah, all the wealth of the city, all its profits, all its prized belongings, and all its treasures. He asserted that all was under immediate threat by the harsh judgment of God.

That abrasive exchange brings us to our text in chapter 20. I settled on this sequence because in the company of pastors and priests—it could be any of us—we all know about saying a word and being labeled an enemy of all that is treasured, if not arrested, then isolated, if not publicly scorned, then at least a subject of many monstrous rumors, much gossip, and canceled pledges. And all because one is boldly faithful, reasonably faithful in the service of one's call, but perceived by others as an enemy of all that is precious.

This sermon is only for those among us who find ourselves in conflict, under assault, in deep tension for the practice of faith. It is for you, even if you have not been publicly humiliated with stocks in the public square. But it is only for those few among us in such dispute. Others of you may listen or leave, but it is not for you.

I

The narrative sequence of prophetic declaration, arrest, and invective intensified the dispute in Jerusalem and caused the zealous prophet to sink into deep turmoil and doubt, leaving us with questions: What should happen next in the text? What word should come next in the text? Well, the editors of the book of Jeremiah have decided what comes next, and it strikes me as a good decision. After the harsh public exchange, the break from the narrative in 20:6 to the poem in 20:7 is an abrupt move from public dispute to Jeremiah at prayer. It is in prayer that this man of deep dispute finds sustenance for his life and his ministry; he finds sustenance, however, only by continued dispute, this time in secret. Only this time it is dispute with the God who has called him into this unbearable ministry in the first place.

II

I have always read Jesus' injunction to us in the Sermon on the Mount as an imperative to privacy, in order to avoid high phrases and ostentatious spirituality. Maybe that is what Jesus intends. He said, as you know:

> But whenever you pray, go into your room and shut the door and pray to your Father who is in secret; and your Father who sees in secret will reward you. When you are praying, do not heap up empty phrases as the Gentiles do, for they think that they will be heard because of their many words. (Matt 6:6-7)

When the teaching of Jesus on prayer is connected to the crisis of Jeremiah, however, a different thought occurs to me. Maybe the reason for prayer in secret, rather than the danger of public display, is that Jeremiah is about to get down and dirty with the God who calls him. Jeremiah must pray in secret, not because to pray in public is a temptation to ostentatiousness as much as it is that such prayer in public would be a scandal to both prophet and God, for things must be said that are not for the curious, censorious ears of Pashur. Jesus says do it in secret:

> Go to your room and shut the door and pray to your Father who is in secret; and your Father who sees in secret will reward you.

This is the one from whom no secret can be hid!

But the secret that cannot be hid from the Father is not that one has a big wish list to speak to the hearer of our prayers. Nor is the secret that Jeremiah has deep sins about which God already knows. Not petition and not confession, but simply the transaction of genuine, honest dialogue with no holds barred, a dialogue upon which life depends and upon which ministry must be premised. I propose that it is this secret exchange with no holds barred that is the secret of survival for this Jeremiah whose very survival is at risk because of the accusatory onslaught of the establishment. My thought in this sermon is a simple one: the public ministry of Jeremiah 20:1-6 (including his arrest and humiliation) is juxtaposed to the prayer of 20:7-13 because it is *secret prayer* that permits energy, freedom, and courage for *public ministry*.

The servants who faithfully show God to the world are those who live in deep, disputatious conversation with God. I think this is worth talking about because I believe faithful ministry in time to come will be increasingly a contested practice that will test our faith and require both every resource we can muster and every resource that God will give us. The ultimate resource for ministry, I propose, is honest conversation with God through which God is drawn, deep and thick, into the needfulness of our ministry. So consider this prayer, which rendered Jeremiah bold and fearless in public places.

III

The prayer begins in truth-telling against God, *a bold accusation* that borders on paranoia:

> O LORD, you have enticed me,
>   and I was enticed;
> You have overpowered me,
>   and you have prevailed.
> I have become a laughingstock all day long;
>   everyone mocks me. (v. 7)

Strong language this. The God who called the prophet is a trickster who has lured him into vocation under false pretenses. Along with wile, this calling God has coerced and forced, and left the prophet with no alternative. Jeremiah had protested against the call at the outset, but God would not be persuaded otherwise. As a result, Jeremiah is forced to become this voice that warns, accuses, exposes, and undermines in Jerusalem. He had said, in his vivid imagery, that his society is on the way to death by its foolish choices that lead to foolish, God-defying policies. That is all that he had said; but he had to say it.

The vocation is too hard. But it turns out that the prophet has only two choices:

> For whenever I speak, I must cry out,
>   I must shout, "Violence and destruction!"
> For the word of the LORD has become for me
>   a reproach and derision all day long.
> If I say, "I will not mention him,
>   or speak any more in his name,"
> then within me there is something like a burning fire
>   shut up in my bones;
> I am weary with holding it in,
>   and I cannot.
> For I hear many whispering:
>   "Terror is all around!
> Denounce him! Let us denounce him!"
>   All my close friends are watching for me to stumble.
> "Perhaps he can be enticed,
>   and we can prevail against him,
>   and take our revenge on him." (vv. 8-10)

Two choices: either he can *speak*, and that leads to all kinds of hostility and alienation, rejection by close friends, rejection on every side; or he can *be silent,* and then the stuff burns on the inside. Either speech or silence. Either way unbearable, all because of the seductive God of Israel who has forced him into an impossible vocation. Better not to have been called; better not to notice or to care. But now all those options are gone; the poet has run out of options. The God who promised to support him is no support at all; that God is fickle and now must listen to this assault of prayer . . . all in secret, no holds barred, down and dirty. The prayer is in secret, the text is unsuspected by his contemporaries, the intensity is unrecognized, all necessary to survival, but in secret.

IV

But then a reversal of sentiment. In public one must be consistent, coherent, measured. In secret, however, one can be as self-contradictory and herky-jerky as one's teeming, self-contradictory emotions require. This God accused is *the God to be trusted,* because the prophet is innocent, has kept his call, and so counts completely upon this harsh God to be ally and guardian:

> But the LORD is with me like a dread warrior;
>   therefore my persecutors will stumble,
>   and they will not prevail.
> They will be greatly shamed,
>   for they will not succeed.
> Their eternal dishonor
>   will never be forgotten.
> O LORD of hosts, you test the righteous,
>   you see the heart and the mind:
> let me see your retribution upon them,
>   for to you I have committed my cause. (vv. 11-12)

This God is still ferocious, still powerful, still overriding, only now as Jeremiah's ally. This is the God who prevailed over Jeremiah. And now Jeremiah is utterly certain that none of his enemies can prevail, precisely because God is dread warrior who will withstand every onslaught. For a moment God was enemy; in that moment when all were enemy. But when Jeremiah remembers clearly that his enemy is Pashur, that sacral bureaucrat and the men of Anathoth, he is able to acknowledge God, in his desperate prayer, as a friend and ally.

God is trustworthy, strong but not fickle. This is the very God to whom prayers can be reliably made, not a nice God, not a therapeutic God, not a warm fuzzy, not a dear uncle, but God of hosts, God with hard capacities and stern resolves. Jeremiah prays to and trusts this God, because he himself cannot withstand his persecutors, and he will not appeal to a God who is kind but helpless.

> So in secret he prays to this God,
> who will do for him what he cannot do for himself,
> who will prevail for him against every enemy threat,
> who will remember the shame of the adversary,
> who will work retaliation upon the enemy.

This *desperate man* has become this *confident man* through this secret negotiation in which the truth is told. Jeremiah had not needed to be polite or consistent, and now does not need to be modest or gentle. It is in secret and so he can move to the deepest extremity of confidence, a confidence adequate even for his desperate social context.

V

Accusation turns to *confidence*. And now in verse 13 *confidence* turns to glad, yielding *praise:*

> Sing to the Lord;
>   praise the Lord!
> For he has delivered the life of the needy
>   from the hands of evildoers.

What a voice! Who would have thought in verse 7 that Jeremiah would get to that cadence of doxology! No doubt he is still surrounded by evildoers like Pashur who would like to put him permanently in stocks . . . or worse. No doubt he will soon have to go back into the fray, out beyond his closet of secret prayer, for that is his calling and he cannot duck it. He now does not want to duck it; he now knows that if he ducks it he will get acute heartburn "like a burning fire shut up in my bones." Still the same role, still the same adversaries, but new in God, now assured yet again that the God who calls is the God who delivers all the needy, but particularly delivers this needy prophet who has no other resource.

The dramatic turn in this verse is astonishing. How did Jeremiah make that move? Well, perhaps God came to him somewhere in the midst of this poem, reiterating the assurance, "I am with you." Such dramatic reentry by God, however, is only possible for the public prophet who practices a second, hidden life of faith. In that hidden life of faith, the prophet is not advocate, not shrill moralist, not cocksure about the great public issues, but rather is down and dirty, down and dirty enough to learn again that the God who calls and lures and avenges is not the God of social action or covenantal Torah or righteous indignation, but is the down and dirty God with whom talk must be daring, who must be assaulted and challenged and resisted and defied . . . and eventually praised. So this text and this sermon are for pastors for whom life is unbearable in stress and tension. The text is an assertion that for all the coping techniques of stress management and time management and support groups . . . all important in themselves . . . that in the end the issue is an intimate theological one. There must be deep *freedom in secret* with the holy, calling God in order that there be *deep courage in public ministry*. Without such secret, the public practice becomes one of cynicism or accommodation or a dozen other forms of fickleness.

I must be honest enough to tell you that if you read past verse 13 into verses 14-18, the prophet immediately falls out of doxology into what sounds like despair and depression. It would be better if doxology was the final word and the chapter ended in verse 13. But of course doxology never is the final word. After doxology there is always the deep reality of intransigence that talks us out of praise and into self-pity. Of course. That reality is known to every person called of this God.

Clearly, however, the depth of verses 14-18 is also not final. Jeremiah moves past that as well. For he is soon back after that again into fierce confrontation about the truth that must be told. He moves past despair because he now has resources. He has the God who calls him, the promise of presence, and the chance to go back to verse 7 and say it all again, always again, and arriving always again at a moment of doxology. What we know in ministry is that we never arrive. We just stay at it and do it again. We do it again in public. But we do it in public because we do it in secret. We move back and forth. We survive . . . just barely . . . but we survive.

VI

There was good reason for Jesus to say what he did about prayer. Prayer in public is too polite for those who find themselves in deep vocations. We may find the shrewdness of Jesus seconded by the poetic imagination of John Donne. He offers as a prayer:

> Batter my heart, three-personed God; for You
> As yet but knock, breathe, shine, and seek to mend;
> That I may rise and stand, O'erthrow me, and bend
> Your force to break, blow, burn, and make me new.
> I, like an usurped town, to'another due,
> labor to admit You, But O, to no end;
> Reason, your viceroy in me, me should defend,
> But is captive, and proves weak or untrue.
> yet dearly I love you and would be loved fain,

But am betrothed unto your enemy.
Divorce me, untie or break that knot again;
Take me to you, imprison me, for I,
Except you enthrall me, never shall be free,
Nor ever chaste, except you ravish me. (sonnet 14)

The very God who puts us in harm's way is the one to whom we turn in deepest intimacy, there in servitude to be set free, there to be healed, healed and imprisoned, drawn to rage and resentment, seeking for revenge, rising to praise, all moments of real life given us in secret with our secret enemy become the one who loves us most deeply and most dearly.

The news is that *survival* is *a secret art*. It depends upon renderings that are honest, conflicted, ragged, and lyrical. We are offered such a secret of survival, and then back to the public place. We go there on behalf of the God who promised at the outset:

> But you, gird up your loins; stand up and tell them everything that I command you. Do not break down before them, or I will break you before them. And I for my part have made you today a fortified city, an iron pillar, and a bronze wall, against the whole land—against the kings of Judah, its princes, its priests, and the people of the land. They will fight against you; but they shall not prevail against you, for I am with you, says the LORD, to deliver you. (Jer 1:17-19)

Jeremiah can remember that initial assurance and prays it back to God with confidence:

> But the LORD is with me like a dread warrior;
> > therefore my persecutors will stumble,
> > and they will not prevail. (20:11)

Praise will not last, cannot last. But it is a treasured moment, a nervy assertion. Jeremiah gives thanks for life given again:

> Sing praise to the LORD;
> > praise the LORD!

For he has delivered the life of the needy
  from the hands of evildoers. (20:13)

His prayer is part of the larger prayer of hope that the church and all
its pastors sing in the face of evil:

The kingdom of the world has become the kingdom of our
  Lord
  and of his Messiah,
and he will reign forever and ever. (Rev 11:15)

Secret survival, public ministry, large hope, sure promise, and all the
while truth-telling . . . enough to keep going, again and again, and
going and going and going.

Fourth Presbyterian Church in Chicago, Illinois / May 21, 2002
Festival of Homiletics

On Reading Jeremiah 1

You, dread warrior on the march,
You, lurking tiger, ready to spring,
You, provoked potter against recalcitrant clay;
     We approach you at the outset of this day.

And while we do,
     we watch the old powers, church and state,
          fall apart and cling desperately to
               what was and what will not be.

     We notice the seeping away of what is treasured among us,
          and in our eager anxiety seek to hold back the loss.
     We sense bewilderment on every side,
          to which we ourselves are more than a little participant.

Grant us courage this day,
     that while we watch,
     and while we notice
     and while we sense,
we may read our world rightly while we stand in your presence,
     that we may discern your complicity in the loss,
     that we may trust your terror to be purposeful,
     that we may imagine the loss birthed to goodness
          that we cannot see or conjure for ourselves.

Stay nearby, you in your terror, and be gracious;
     you in your lurking, be patient;
     you in your provocation, make this weary world new,
          alive in praise to you. Amen.

June 17, 2002 (Montreat)

Variations from the Barrio

Exodus 1:15-22; Exodus 15:20-21; 1 Corinthians 1:24-29

It required considerable anguish for this aging white guy to dare to speak in the midst of the magic worked by Dwight Andrews. Anguish, because I only know three things about jazz:

1. Jazz arises among the disadvantaged who cannot afford to have things settled because they will always settle against them. And so they practice a beat that keeps moving, keeps upsetting, keeps subverting, keeps making impossible angles of reality possible and available. The disadvantaged patrons of jazz always come from and live in some barrio or another, far from settled power, if not a barrio, a slum, if not a slum, some other arena of marginality where one dare not even hope for comfortable settlement.

2. Jazz consists in a theme that keeps recurring.

3. That theme is played out with endless variations, enormous freedom, but under discipline to the core theme to which reference is endlessly made, return to which always matters decisively.

That is the sum of what this lead-footed white man knows about jazz. I will see if that is enough to last for these twenty minutes or so.

I

So consider *the natural habitat of jazz in the barrio.* Jazz does not arise among tenured whites, not even among privileged blacks, but among those who go for broke every time because there is so little to lose, so much to hear and say, so much to hope. Behind Dwight and his company are the long history of New Orleans and perhaps also my hometowns of St. Louis and Kansas City. But we go back further than those old, weary cities. We go back to the Easter dances of those who saw up close the Dead One raised to power. But behind Easter we go way back to Daniel and we watch the three Jewish boys kept safe while they danced on hot coals in the furnace of Nebuchadnezzar, dancing safe and not burning (Dan 3:27-28). But we go behind the furnace to the exile where our folks sang songs of remembered Zion, which the Babylonians and many other managers mocked and teased, but the songs would not cease (Ps 137:1-6). But we can go back behind exile far enough back to David the eighth son, the little runt of a king moved to power, unafraid in his innocence to dance before the invisible God who sat on the ark, and we watch the runt take office (1 Sam 16:12-13; 2 Sam 6:16). But we go behind David and behind and behind.

If you keep pushing back you will come to the very bottom of the story of jazz. It is told in Exodus 1, told in the midst of a Pharaoh whose name we cannot remember, because if you have seen one Pharaoh, you have seen them all. This nameless "Lord of Egypt" who tries to stop the music, decrees a big killing of all of the dangerous sons of freedom (Exod 1:16). Then with Pharaoh's name erased, we learn of two mothers in the barrio who feared God and defied Pharaoh and birthed futures (Exod 1:17). They were shrewdly deferential toward pernicious Pharaoh, but if a slave you can appear deferential and, at the same time, bring the babies and futures out to life. Wonder of wonders we know their names: Shiphrah and Puah (Exod 1:15)! They are Hebrew midwives, down in the slave huts, birthing sons and daughters. We forgot the name of Pharaoh; we passionately remember the mothers of our future! Pharaoh was utterly surprised by their nerve and their success; he noticed the slave huts teeming with life. He watched the slave camp grow big and dangerous in free- dom. Shiphrah and Puah took the new babies and, like a scene from Toni Morrison, they danced the children of freedom around the bricks and around the clay and by the straw; they danced all night even until sun-up. Because of their singing the Hebrew barrio became a future-infested place from which has arisen all the later daring dances of freedom, a dance of defiance and gratitude and hope. The babies watched the women that day. They looked to the edge of the campsite and they saw the new land of freedom and peace and justice and well-being just coming into view. They were able to see, because their lens of observation was peopled by the dancing feet of those who refused the settlement of Pharaoh.

II

The barrio kept tapping to a future and swaying to God's newness. Shiphrah and Puah encouraged the babies to sing and clap and vibrate. All the movement of their bodies was scary to Pharaoh who got really crazy, not used to seeing midwives buoyant and unsubmissive. The two women fashioned the song; the women and children kept humming it. The song picked up momentum when it was rumored that by the third plague the Egyptians could not make gnats (Exod 8:18). And then even Pharaoh became nervous and asked Moses to forgive him (Exod 10:16-17). The song just kept on, they holding the tambourines high above the waters. They moved beyond all their fears and all the old tired threats of the empire that were no longer credible.

They reached the other side and they immediately began a debate about the proper response to the miracle of the freedom. Aaron the priest wanted to offer sacrifices. Moses wanted to discuss the rules for the coming revolution. But their sister, Miriam, long associated with Shiphrah and Puah, had a better idea. Without much planning but with inventive impulses, she grabbed a tambourine. The two other women followed her to the front of the crowd. They shook the tambourines. They laughed. They danced. They sang. And as they sang, they lined out the basic theme that would dominate all the future music in the community. Listen to it:

> *Sing to the* LORD, sing to the LORD of hosts
> *For* . . . because . . . why. Because *the horse*
> (that is the whole imperial army) *and the*
> *rider* (that is the nameless Pharaoh
> who tried to stop the march of freedom),
> *the horse and the rider he has thrown in the sea.*
> The sea is the residue of chaos, the anxious
> power of disorder and darkness. And now
> the newness of life comes midst the dangerous waters,
> because Pharaoh and all his ilk have disappeared
> below the surface of the waters of death.

That is what the women sang in the first hour of freedom. And it has been the song in this barrio community since then:

> Sing to the LORD . . .
> horse and rider he has thrown into the sea. (Exod 15:21)

Finé!—end of empire, end of death, end of brick quotas, end of fear, end of anxiety, end of greed, end of alienation!

This glorious claim for the defeat of the powers of chaos, oppression, and death is *the primal theme of the entire score*. Every jazz player in every barrio after Miriam knows that this main theme cannot vary. Every jazz singer also knows that in every listening assemblage there are those who cannot tolerate that cadence:

> The song of Miriam is no comfort to conservatives who want
> to get frozen into an eternal certitude.
> The song is no comfort to liberals who want to turn everything
> into a cause and think rationally in order to exhibit our
> own great compassion and courage.
> The song is no comfort to those who want to get the church
> straightened out.
> The song is no comfort to whites who want old patterns of
> power and authority to be revived.
> The song is no comfort to blacks who buy in on old power
> arrangements whether as victim or newly as controller.

The song is no comfort to any of our ambitions, precisely because the new beat of the barrio jazz is not about us. It is about *the Other One*, this holy God like whom there is no other . . .

> with more power than the empire,
> with more passion than the nursemaids,
> with more wisdom than the learned,
> with more mercy than bleeding heart liberals,

The song is testimony to the one who comes to save, redeem, transform, restore, heal, feed, forgive, cleanse . . . make all things new.

> This is my story, this is my song, this is the noise of our
> tambourine, this is the pattern of our dancing feet, this is
> the beat, this is the way scripture is heard and played and
> performed and enacted in the world.

One theme played over and over and over with amazing variation.

We have been singing the song forever, with endless imagination, daring cadences, open, astonishing surprises, but always returning to the main beat that any child in the barrio can identify promptly.

So consider the variations:

Hannah sang after the unexpected baby was born:

> The LORD kills and brings to life;
> > he brings down to Sheol and raises up.
> The LORD makes poor and makes rich;
> > he brings low, he also exalts.
> He raises up the poor from the dust;
> > he lifts the needy from the ash heap,
> to make them sit with princes
> > and inherit a seat of honor.
> For the pillars of the earth are the LORD's,
> > and on them he has set the world. (1 Sam 2:6-8)

And you can hear Miriam's tambourines with the same beat in the lips of Hannah. *David's* song looks back to a lifetime of unexpected gifts from God:

> Indeed, you are my lamp, O LORD,
> > the LORD lightens my darkness.
> By you I can crush a troop,
> > and by my God I can leap over a wall.
> This God—his way is perfect;
> > the promise of the LORD proves true;
> > he is a shield for all who take refuge in him.
> (2 Sam 22:29-31)

Hezekiah's song arose in gratitude when he was healed as he was about to die:

> The living, the living, they thank you,
> > as I do this day;
> fathers make known to children
> > your faithfulness.

The LORD will save me,
    and we will sing to stringed instruments
all the days of our lives
    at the house of the LORD. (Isa 38:19-20)

Micah ended his poetry in singing:

He will again have compassion upon us;
    he will tread our iniquities under foot.
You will cast all our sins
    into the depths of the sea.
You will show faithfulness to Jacob
    and unswerving loyalty to Abraham,
as you have sworn to our ancestors
    from the days of old. (Mic 7:19-20)

Habakkuk put it another way:

Though the fig tree does not blossom,
    and no fruit is on the vines;
though the produce of the olive fails,
    and the fields yield no food;
though the flock is cut off from the fold,
    and there is no herd in the stalls,
yet I will rejoice in the LORD;
    I will exult in the God of my salvation. (Hab 3:17-18)

After a long time *Mother Mary* sang in anticipation, echoing Mother Hannah:

He has brought down the powerful from their thrones,
    and lifted up the lowly;
he has filled the hungry with good things,
    and sent the rich away empty.
He has helped his servant Israel,
    in remembrance of his mercy,
according to the promise he made to our ancestors,
    to Abraham and to his descendants forever.
    (Luke 1:52-55)

Jesus lined out the news in his own familiar words:

> No one can serve two masters; for a slave will either hate the one and love the other, or be devoted to the one and despise the other. You cannot serve God and wealth. Therefore I tell you, do not worry about your life, what you will eat or what you will drink, or about your body, what you will wear. Is not life more than food, and the body more than clothing? (Matt 6:24-25)

> Come to me, all you that are weary and are carrying heavy burdens, and I will give you rest. Take my yoke upon you, and learn from me; for I am gentle and humble in heart, and you will find rest for your souls. For my yoke is easy, and my burden is light. (Matt 11:28-30)

> Then he said to them, "The sabbath was made for humankind and not humankind for the sabbath; so the Son of Man is lord even of the sabbath." (Mark 2:27-28)

And then *Paul* in his vigorous cadences:

> O the depth of the riches and wisdom and knowledge of God! How unsearchable are his judgments and how inscrutable his ways!
>
> > For who has known the mind of the Lord?
> > Or who has been his counselor?
> > Or who has given a gift to him,
> > > to receive a gift in return?
>
> For from him and through him and to him are all things. To him be the glory forever. Amen. (Rom 11:33-36)

And then *Paul* again:

> For I am convinced that neither death, nor life, nor angels, nor rulers, nor things present, nor things to come, nor powers, nor height, nor depth, nor anything else in all creation, will be able to separate us from the love of God in Christ Jesus our Lord. (Rom 8:38-39)

And then *Paul* yet one more time:

> Death has been swallowed up in victory.
> Where, O death, is your victory?
> Where, O death, is your sting? (1 Cor 15:54b-55)

And then just beyond Paul *a great few* give memory of the church:

> All of these died in faith without having received the
> promises, but from a distance they saw and greeted them.
> They confessed that they were strangers and foreigners
> on the earth, for people who speak in this way make it
> clear that they are seeking a homeland. If they had been
> thinking of the land that they had left behind, they would
> have had opportunity to return. But as it is, they desire a
> better country, that is, a heavenly one. Therefore God is
> not ashamed to be called their God; indeed, he has pre-
> pared a city for them. (Heb 11:13-16)

And the last word goes to *the last writer:*

> The kingdom of the world has become the kingdom of our
>   Lord
>   and of his Messiah,
> and he will reign forever and ever. (Rev 11:15)

Now you know all of this. I tell it to you for one reason only, that
you may observe that not one of these great jazz artists in our past has
moved a cubit away from the sounds of Miriam. Miriam herself could
pick up the beat from any one of these later voices and return to the
initial score. The women with the tambourine at the waterside, in the
company of Shiphrah and Puah, could lead the next sixteen measures
of whatever it is that comes next in this inventive song.

The beat comes out of the barrio because the force is with us. The
theme arises from the sisters' tambourines because God is faithful.
Endless variation comes in many places and in many times, but never
far from the theme. We have a name for the barrio theme in its endless
variations. It is "news," "gospel," the truth of God that impinges upon
the world come close in Jesus, treasured in word and sacrament, evident in bold walk and cared for in disciplined talk. And the outcome

is a people alert to Pharaoh, but having laughed an Easter laugh . . .
utterly unafraid.

<h2 style="text-align:center">IV</h2>

All good news. But now a sober thought about which Dwight might
wonder because jazz never stops for a sober thought:

What has happened to this dear people of God that has grown old
to the news of God's rescue?!

- we nickel and dime,
- we settle for committees,
- we pester to balance races,
- we doubt, and in doubt grow weary and in weariness become
  fearful and anxious and ambitious.

Well, in the face of all of the resilience of the beat and even despite the
endless variation, Miriam's lead theme still matters.

- If you think you are smart enough to have it your own way,
  consider your call.
- If you think you know how to muscle your way ahead of
  all the others,
  consider your call.
- If you think you have privilege because you come from
  somewhere special,
  consider your call.

> Consider your own call, brothers and sisters: not many of
> you were wise by human standards, not many were pow-
> erful, not many were of noble birth. But God chose what
> is foolish in the world to shame the wise; God chose what
> is weak in the world to shame the strong; God chose what
> is low and despised in the world, things that are not, to
> reduce to nothing things that are, so that no one might
> boast in the presence of God. (1 Cor 1:26-29)

This is a time when church people must get past themselves, beyond
our pet projects, beyond our treasured controls, beyond our nour-
ished angers, and we know why, because:

For God's foolishness is wiser than human wisdom, and
God's weakness is stronger than human strength.
(1 Cor 1:25)

The world is going to die in its strength. Our society is going to commit disaster in its wisdom. And we, since Shiphrah and Puah, since Miriam, we have found gospel newness:

weakness adequate in the face of deathly strength,
foolishness compelling in the face of destructive wisdom.

It is adequate! It is no wonder that the beat of the first exhibit of news will not stop. It is the truth, but it is not about us. It is about the one who has made all things new, of whom we gladly confess:

The steadfast love of the LORD never ceases,
    his mercies never come to an end;
they are new every morning;
    great is your faithfulness. (Lam 3:22-23)

Shame on us, church, for reducing the lyric of newness to the staleness of our predictable slogans. Shame on us. Listen once more to the beat:

The steadfast love of the LORD never ceases,
    his mercies never come to an end;
they are new every morning;
    great is your faithfulness. (Lam 3:22-23)

Southeast Conference meeting of the UCC / June 14, 2003
in the midst of a jazz vesper led by Dwight Andrews

On 9/11: One Year Later

Rock of Ages, cleft for me,
Let me hide myself in Thee;
Naked, come to Thee for dress,
Helpless, look to Thee for grace;
Be of sin the double cure,
Cleanse me from its guilt and power.

While I draw this fleeting breath,
When my eyelids close in death,
When I soar to worlds unknown,
See thee on Thy judgment throne,
Rock of Ages, cleft for me,
Let me hide myself in Thee.

You rock of strength and power and certitude,
You rock higher than all the waters of chaos,
You shelter safer than all threats,
You dwelling place in all generations,
You who goes before us and is rear guard after us,

We turn to you for safety, security, assurance,
        for we have had a deep fill of alarm,
                                displacement,
                                loss,
                                threat . . .
        all becoming a lingering sense of vulnerability
        new to us, and we grow weary of the risk.

We turn to you in that heaviness,
for we do afresh ponder our mortality,
think about our naked exposure,
fully cognizant of the fragility that is the truth of our lives.
And so we turn to you
seeking assurance, consolation, embrace.

And you receive us, faithful mother who holds
sure father who welcomes and embraces,
And we settle in peaceableness even midst the chaos
we do . . . and we give you thanks.

And then, because of the narrative we know best,
we discover that in the rock where you had
nestled us,
You have blown the rock open from the inside,
You have rolled the stone away,
You have surged out of a tomb-like womb
a womb-like tomb,
And are back surging in the world,
to Jerusalem and Galilee and to parts unknown,
life overriding death,
work overriding dormancy,
risk moving beyond solace . . .
all things new and we ponder our oldest mantra:
"Christ is risen . . . He is risen indeed."

You are risen in power and wonder;
You are risen out of the shambles of death and terror and doubt and
fear;
You are risen to turn the world to peace and justice and freedom and
well-being;
You are risen with healing wings to cure our diseased hurts and our
public pathologies.

You are risen and summoning us,
summoning us beyond our fear to obedience,
summoning us beyond our nestling to freedom,
summoning us beyond our self-preoccupation to courage,

summoning us beyond our safety to your
        bold, transformative way in the world.

We dare imagine that the rock of safety blown open to newness
    matters even to our school.
        So we ask your risen power and
            your stirring spirit among us,
      that our common life may be like bread broken
                in remembering you
                and like wine poured out
                in hope of your coming soon.

Let us, good Lord of the dying and the living,
    hide ourselves in Thee.
And then let us follow your Easter way,
      that the world shriveled in deathliness
           may turn to joy and to newness.

We gladly attest. Christ is Risen
And the congregation answers. "He is risen indeed!"
                       Amen.

Columbia Theological Seminary chapel service / September 11, 2002

Shrill Faith for the Nighttime

Psalm 30:4-11; Luke 18:1-8

You will recall that President Gerald Ford, when he became president after the long process of expelling Richard Nixon from the presidency, said—in his first public utterance as president—"America's long nightmare is over." He meant that we could move on and restore civic life. It interests me greatly that he used the image of "nightmare" for that national trauma, an image that gives me a beginning point for my words to you.

I

Nighttime is an odd time in human life, indicated by the fact that young children never want to go to bed. It is a scary time. It is a time out of control, plus the fact that you might miss something. In the daytime, before we go to bed, we mostly manage and cope, and even do well, and stay in control of our lives as best we can. When we wake up the next morning, we may sleep late or get up early; but either way, we take on the day and pick up our activities and responsibilities and cope, more-or-less as best we can.

But in between going to bed and waking up, there is that odd time when we let our guard down. We can't help it. We let our guard down because, as we say, we "lose consciousness." In an age before electricity, it was a very dark time and the forces beyond our control—either real or imagined—crowded in our lives. That is why ghosts and spooks operate at night, out of control, when we cannot see them. That is why, moreover, the pivotal events in biblical faith happen at nighttime, when we cannot see them. Specifically, the deliverance of Israel from Egypt happened at night and the resurrection of Jesus from the dead happened at night when no one saw. All of us, moreover, know about the night when we hear strange noises and our anxieties become large, and we go over and over and over things that are beyond our control. Sigmund Freud, of course, made a defining

179

study of dreams; he understood that in dreams unexpected and sometimes unwelcome messages come to us that have force and meaning, often embodying those parts of our life that we do not understand or control. Unlike the daytime, the nighttime is *vulnerable* and *exposed* and *dangerous*. It is that time when we cannot manage, and people of faith are drawn to God as a source of safety when there is no other source of safety, and as a source of presence when the world feels absent.

And now, nightmares are very big in our world . . . wars and rumors of war and terror and assault and threat and violence. We feel unsafe and we dream up all kinds of security programs that do not in fact make us any safer, but if anything, only more anxious. Daytime is for *obedience and virtue and morality*. But nighttime is for *threat and danger and anxiety*.

II

In this sermon, I want to think about the special, mostly neglected resources of faith given in the Bible for the nighttime when we are under threat. I want to consider with you one psalm in which the psalmist tells about his own crisis of faith. And of course the reason we pay attention to this particular experience of that ancient psalmist, and the reason his experience got into the Bible, is because that experience of faith reported here is so very like our own.

Psalm 30 is like a "journal" of *two days and one night* in the stressful reality of faith. I share this psalm with you because it seems clear that the Bible has resources that are much needed in our time of great societal nightmare.

The speaker of Psalm 30 is a person of immense faith and is eager to share that faith. In introductory comments, the speaker says, "I want you all to join in songs of faith with me":

> Sing praises to the LORD, O you his faithful ones,
> and give thanks to his holy name. (Ps 30:4)

Everyone must join in this song. And here is the reason:

> For God's anger is but for a moment;
> his favor is for a lifetime.
> Weeping may linger for the night,
> but joy comes with the morning. (Ps 30:5)

God does indeed get angry, and that causes alienation. But God's anger is brief; in Hebrew the word is "like a beat"! That is compared to God's favor toward us that lasts a lifetime, much, much longer than the anger, and that is cause for celebration. Indeed, sadness and weeping might last through the night, but then comes joy.

So the speaker makes four contrasts:

anger	favor
beat	a lifetime
sorrow	joy
night	morning

The bad stuff is real, and the psalmist does not deny that. But the bad stuff that is real is not the last thing, because the last thing is the light of morning that God reliably gives that overrides every season of nightmare. That is the theme of the psalm, but then the speaker goes back over it in greater detail.

III

The speaker says, *"Let me tell you about the first day* of this tale. It was a great day. I was on top of the world, everything was good, everything was right, 'all things were bright and beautiful'"*:

> As for me, I said in my prosperity,
>   "I shall never be moved."
> By your favor, O LORD,
>   you had established me as a strong mountain. (Ps 30:6-7a)

"I was so confident of a good job, good family, good house, good education, good healthcare, good income. I was so confident that I said, not meaning to brag, 'I will never be tottered,' never be shaken or made unstable. That is what I said as I went to bed. I was so happy and I was so sure and I was so grateful to God."

IV

But then, says the speaker, *"Let me tell you about the night.* All of a sudden, just as night came, right in the middle of verse 7, without explanation, trouble came just when I was so cocky." It happened that day, all at once and the world came crumbling down:

- a pink slip
- a pregnant teenager
- a cancer diagnosis
- a terrorist attack
- an Enron debacle
- an old secret exposed to shameful light.

And there is a flood of vexed feeling. The psalmist says it this way:

> you hid your face;
>> I was dismayed. (Ps 30:7b)

The biblical way of talking is that we live because God's face shines upon us, or as we say, "The LORD bless you and keep you and cause his face to shine upon you." It is the way of a small child who is frantic but is suddenly okay when she sees her mother's face. But if mother turns away or is absent or is unavailable or is unresponsive, the world is immediately a place of threat. When God's face of blessing was hidden, "I was in dismay."

What to do in the nightmare? Well, this is a person of faith. And what the faithful know to do is to *pray vigorously,* to *summon* God, to *address urgent imperatives* to God, confident that even in the night, the God beyond all nightmares is reachable. This is what the psalmist says:

> To you, O LORD, I cried,
>> and to the LORD I made supplication: (Ps 30:8)

"I addressed the very God who was absent. I addressed God and I began to dispute with God":

> What profit is there in my death,
>> if I go down to the Pit?
> Will the dust praise you?
>> Will it tell of your faithfulness? (Ps 30:9)

"I made the case to God that letting me die in the night would not do God any good. I took myself to be so important that I reminded God I would be worthless to God if God let me die. Since I sing in the choir, I reminded God that if God lost me, there would be one less singer and that much less praise addressed to God. I pressed God and I appealed to God's self-interest. My prayer was a little manipulative, but I was desperate":

> What profit is there in my death,
>> if I go down to the Pit?
> Will the dust praise you?
>> Will it tell of your faithfulness? (Ps 30:9)

And then I addressed God in heavy, weighty imperatives that I had never dared sound before:

- Hear me
- Be gracious to me
- Be my helper.

I called God by name twice, so that there would be no confusion on God's part that it was this God whom I expected to help me:

> Hear, O LORD, and be gracious to me!
>> O LORD, be my helper!" (Ps 30:10)

I am rather astonished at myself as I think about my prayer, because I never thought I would be so bold and assertive to take the upper hand in the night and insist that God must do what I needed to have done. I would never talk to God that way in the daytime; but in the night, when you are desperate, you can try anything. As soon as I had carried my case to God, I left the problem with God and I went to sleep, confident that God would be at work even in the middle of the night, even in the presence of the nightmare.

V

And then says the psalmist, "I woke up at daybreak." It had been a terrible night, but not as terrible for me as for God. In my anxiety I had given God a huge assignment. My prayer to God was that God deal with the nightmare when I was dismayed. I did not know if God would answer, but I had no alternative. In the daytime, I would have gotten other help; but at night, in the nightmare, clearly God is the only source of help.

So imagine my surprise and my delight when the next day came, and my life had been healed by the hidden work of the God who resolves all nightmares. *Let me tell you about the next morning.* In the morning I gave thanks to God:

> You have turned my mourning into dancing;
>> you have taken off my sackcloth
>> and clothed me with joy,
> so that my soul may praise you and not be silent.
>> O LORD my God, I will give thanks to you forever.
> (Ps 30:11-12)

Think of that! . . .

- mourning to dancing
- funeral clothes to clothes of joy.

A new life—a new day—a new chance. Since that dark night when God overrode the nightmare, my whole life has been a dance of gladness, of endless praise, of endless thanks, of endless well-being, close to God, no longer dismayed.

VI

"I am so glad," says the psalmist, "that I belong to this community of faith that has this pattern of prayer. We are the ones who have a way through beyond nightmares." The way is with a God who has power even in the night, and who hears and who acts, and we find our life transformed.

Says the psalmist, "I am astonished that I spoke to God in such a demanding way: *Hear—be gracious—help me!* All around me are people who say, "Keep your mouth shut and cope and pretend it's okay." But the news that comes clear to me is that if we come boldly to God, strange things happen that cause joy in the morning. "You know," says the psalmist, "my experience is very much like the parable about prayer that Jesus will teach in about five centuries":

> Then Jesus told them a parable about their need to pray always and not to lose heart. (Luke 18:1)

The parable is about a woman who nagged and nagged until the judge gave her a favorable ruling. The point of the parable is to carry the nightmare to God and insist that God should deal with it, and then to trust your life to the God of all nightmares.

If we tough it out in silence, we will lose heart and grow cynical. But Jesus says:

> Pray always . . . and do not lose heart.

That is a good word to a society that is overwhelmed with nightmares:

> Pray always . . . and do not lose heart.

Young Memorial ARP Church, Andersen, South Carolina / September 22, 2002

On Reading Jeremiah 2

You, father of all mercies,
    mother of all light,
    giver of all life,
    ruler of all generous futures:

We approach you in our season of alienation,
        confessing it to be your winter of discontent.

You, father of all mercies,
        now turned hard and impatient
        with children and heirs who have become ungrateful.

You, mother of all light,
        bent now to a season of raging darkness
        with no glimmer of hope beyond.

You, giver of all life, now presiding over such death,
        death among the well-placed as we did not expect,
        death among the refugees we had hardly noticed,
        death by epidemic,
            and by vengeance, remote,
            and by heat, direct,
            almost without notice.

You, ruler of all generous futures,
        but tomorrows now in such short supply:
We mark you by mercy, light, life, future:
    Now shattered beyond expectation;
        should we protest your hard will?

should we doubt you now in dread?
should we confess and own blame?
All of the above . . . none of the above . . . all are bewildered fear,
now ceded to you.

We only know that it is you—not how you receive our fearful prayer,
but *you!*
You are enough and we are yours. Amen.

June 18, 2002 (Montreat)

Bragging about the Right Stuff

Jeremiah 9:23-24; Psalm 87; 1 Corinthians 1:18-31

All great cities brag. They gather their energy, produce their images of success and prosperity, and unleash their propaganda in ads, slogans, and campaigns. They do so because they know, intuitively, that stories of success and prosperity draw people, mobilize resources, generate jobs, accumulate wealth, and eventually—raise the standard of living . . . for some.

I

No great city ever did a better job of bragging than that ancient city of Jerusalem in the Old Testament. Beginning with David and especially with Solomon, Jerusalem gathered its poets and storytellers and liturgists and ad men and sloganeers and made its claim for its urban elite. The bragging took the form of liturgic theology:

> God is our refuge and strength,
>   a very present help in trouble . . .
> God is in the midst of the city;
>   it shall not be moved. (Ps 46:1, 5)

In the psalm we read, it is claimed that:

> Glorious things of thee are spoken,
>   O city of God. (Ps 87:3)

The glorious things are spoken of God . . . the one who lives and saves and guards and protects and guarantees. But when they said glorious things of God, they also said glorious things of the city:

- This is the city of God;
- This is the place of the temple;

- This is the seat of the king;
- This is the place where are gathered all hopes and fears;
- This is the place of promises . . . all will be well.

II

Every great city brags, because it knows that self-celebration enhances life and produces a high standard of living for some. Every great city brags:

- Atlanta, a city too busy to hate
- If you are tired of London, you are tired of life
- Chicago, Chicago, what a wonderful town
- Wonderful, wonderful Copenhagen
- Leave your heart in San Francisco
- How will you keep them down on the farm once they have seen Paris?
- New York, New York, the city that doesn't sleep . . .

Glorious things of thee are spoken, Zion, city of our God! Glorious things of thee are spoken, Atlanta, London, Chicago, Copenhagen, San Francisco, Paris, Atlanta, Jerusalem, Atlanta. Glorious things!

No great city ever did a better job of bragging than that ancient city of Jerusalem in the Old Testament. Beginning with David and especially with Solomon, Jerusalem gathered its poets and storytellers and liturgists and ad men and sloganeers and made its claim for its urban elite. The bragging took the form of liturgic theology:

> God is our refuge and strength,
>   a very present help in trouble. (Ps 46:1)

> God is in the midst of the city;
>   it shall not be moved. (Ps 46:5)

In the psalm we read (87), it is claimed that:

> Glorious things of thee are spoken,
>   O city of God. (Ps 87:3)

The glorious things are spoken of God . . . the one who lives and saves and guards and protects and guarantees. But when they said glorious things of God, they also said glorious things of the city. It is no wonder the wise men in Matthew came looking for the Messiah, the wave of the future, in Jerusalem:

> In the time of King Herod, after Jesus was born in Bethlehem of Judea, wise men from the East came to Jerusalem, asking, "Where is the child who has been born king of the Jews? For we observed his star at its rising, and have come to pay him homage." (Matt 2:1-2)

The wise men had heard all those glorious things. They came, like tribal peasants in South Africa following the light to Johannesburg, sure that they would find there jobs and housing and well-being. It belongs to the great city, or so the great city says in its endless frenzy of self-promotion. All great cities brag about themselves . . . endlessly . . . to the advantage of some.

III

It is likely that Psalm 87 comes early in the Israelite history of Jerusalem, perhaps from the liturgic committees of Solomon in 950 B.C.E. After that, the city had had a rather mixed history:

- It had had an invasion from Egypt under Shishak;
- It had been besieged by Sennacherib and the Assyrians;
- It had seen a series of minor wars with petty neighbors, Northern Israel and Syria;
- It had had a series of bad kings and consequent coups;
- It had had prophets arise who summoned the city back to its senses;
- It had had a couple of good kings, only a couple, Hezekiah and Josiah.

And then, after 400 years, about 600 B.C.E., came Jeremiah. He was a villager who lived just to the north of the city. He and his family before him had watched the city through its 400 years of misconduct and bad policy and mixed success. He had listened to the temple liturgy and he no doubt knew Psalm 87, and,

Psalm 84: "How lovely are thy dwelling places"

Psalm 46: "God is our refuge and help"

Psalm 48:
Walk about Zion, go all around it,
    count its towers,
consider well its ramparts;
    go through its citadels,
that you may tell the next generation
    that this is God,
our God forever and ever.
    He will be our guide forever. (Ps 48:12-14)

Jeremiah had noticed the use of the word "forever," a pretentious liturgical term assuring that the way it is, is the way it will be, the grand illusion of the successful and the prosperous about an absolute present tense.

Jeremiah watched, until he could keep silent no longer. And then he commented on urban bragging. He knew that all great cities bragged, but he wished that Jerusalem would not brag about that sorry stuff. He offered a simple triad of bad bragging:

Do not let the wise boast of their wisdom.
Do not let the mighty boast of their might.
Do not let the wealthy boast of their wealth.

But all great cities boast of *wisdom, might, and wealth*. That triad is what makes a city great.

So imagine that ancient city of Jerusalem—or this contemporary city—bragging about its *wisdom*. Jerusalem would do so by reference to Solomon, the king who was said to be learned and wise in every way:

God gave Solomon very great wisdom, discernment, and breadth of understanding as vast as the sand on the sea-shore, so that Solomon's wisdom surpassed the wisdom of all the people of the east, and all the wisdom of Egypt. (1 Kgs 4:29-30)

He composed three thousand proverbs, and his songs numbered a thousand and five. He would speak of trees, from the cedar that is in the Lebanon to the hyssop that grows in the wall; he would speak of animals, and birds, and reptiles, and fish. People came from all the nations to hear the wisdom of Solomon; they came from all the kings of the earth who had heard of his wisdom.

(1 Kgs 4:32-34)

Solomon was wise enough to know and so to control, for he knew that "knowledge is power." He knew it . . . in downtown Jerusalem! But we are no different. We are so glad for the research universities, so glad for corporate efforts at research and development, research that is never innocent but always in some interest, sometimes business, sometimes government, most often the military. Because economic advance does not come with stupidity or foolishness, but through the awareness of how the world works, and one needs a quota of the wise, the "stars" of the intellectual world, in order to stay ahead and grow.

So imagine, second, the ancient city of Jerusalem or—this contemporary city—bragging about its *might*. In the city we may boast of economic power and growth that, alas, invites new roads. Or we may brag about sports teams, only not just now in Atlanta, because it takes powerful sports teams—with the ensuing sex and violence—to be a world-class city. But urban culture is larger than the city. And eventually might comes to the military. For it is the city that needs the army to protect its banks and the great concentrations of wealth and advantage and high standard of living that others want in on. So Solomon had might to match his wisdom:

He made three hundred shields of beaten gold; three minas of gold went into each shield; and the king put them in the House of the Forest of Lebanon. The king also made a great ivory throne, and overlaid it with the finest gold. The throne had six steps. The top of the throne was rounded in the back, and on each side of the seat were arm rests and two lions standing beside the arm rests. (1 Kgs 10:17-19)

> For the king had a fleet of ships of Tarshish at sea with the
> fleet of Hiram. Once every three years the fleet of the
> ships of Tarshish used to come bringing gold, silver,
> ivory, apes, and peacocks. (1 Kgs 10:22)

And we in our might, so mighty that we "fly over," but get Canadians
and Brits to do the ground war for us, because we are mighty enough
that others will do our dirty work.

So imagine, third, that ancient city of Jerusalem—or this contemporary city—bragging about its *wealth*. Solomon's wealth came because
he controlled the land bridge at the Fertile Crescent and stood at the
center of the global economy:

> Thus King Solomon excelled all the kings of the earth in
> riches and in wisdom. The whole earth sought the pres-
> ence of Solomon to hear his wisdom, which God had put
> into his mind. Every one of them brought a present,
> objects of silver and gold, garments, weaponry, spices,
> horses, and mules, so much year by year. Solomon gath-
> ered together chariots and horses; he had fourteen hun-
> dred chariots and twelve thousand horses, which he
> stationed in the chariot cities and with the king in
> Jerusalem. The king made silver as common in Jerusalem
> as stones, and he made cedars as numerous as the
> sycamores of the Shephelah. (1 Kgs 10:23-27)

If only it weren't for Charlotte, Atlanta could brag more about the
Southeast, its Fortune 500 world headquarters, and our special share
of the Gross National Product, and better jobs and more growth, and
the "New South," and the matrix so much of the world economy, etc.,
etc., etc.

Three things, said Jeremiah, not to brag on: By now you know the
mantra:

> Do not let the wise boast of their wisdom.
> Do not let the mighty boast of their might.
> Do not let the wealthy boast of their wealth.

They are three items but really all one—one by convergence to have
autonomy and the world on our own terms. Solomon has become a

metaphor in that ancient world for wisdom, might, and wealth. So big, so impressive, so proud, so independent, so safe, so happy. And Jeremiah said:

> Do not let the wise boast of their wisdom.
> Do not let the mighty boast of their might.
> Do not let the wealthy boast of their wealth.

IV

Well, they must have answered Jeremiah in indignation: "Don't you think we should brag, given who we are?" And he answered, apparently without blinking, "Yes, you can brag, but you might not want to brag on wisdom, might, and wealth." And they said, "What else is there to brag on?" And he answered, apparently having his response at the ready:

> Let those who boast boast in this, that they understand
> and know me, that I am the LORD; I act with steadfast
> love, justice, and righteousness in the earth, for in these
> things I delight, says the LORD. (Jer 9:24)

His is a quick, terse response. Jeremiah gives Jerusalem another triad for bragging. Brag that you know YHWH, the God of the covenant. This God delights in:

steadfast love, justice, righteousness

Brag about the things that please the God of Israel:

Brag about *steadfast love,* about staying power and keeping vows and promises, about long-term fidelity whereby haves and have-nots, rich and poor, and black and white stay with each other in a common destiny because there are no private deals, no gated communities that can be safe, no private schools that can opt out, no protected oases because all are bound to all, even as God is bound to Israel.

Brag about *justice,* about the practice of economic viability in which the great money revenues of the most fabulous wealth in the world is put to use for all the neighbors in terms of health care, adequate housing, childcare, good schools—all readily doable when the Body Politic comes to know that we are all in it together, that justice is the willingness to submit the economy to the requirements of the neighborhood, in which must some cap their income and their leisure and their self-indulgence in order that all may live well.

Brag about *righteousness,* a vision of a society in viable, sustainable equilibrium, a harmony of neighbors in which none need to be gouging and threatening others and none need be fearful, because common joy and common hope are rooted in common shalom.

V

Well, Jeremiah must have taken their breath away with such a simple, all-comprehending contrast:

> Not brag: *wisdom, might, wealth*
> Brag: *steadfast love, justice, righteousness*

The practice of the second triad is of course complicated, but the agenda is clean and simple, and rooted in the reality of God among us.

Jeremiah knows that the city is destined to failure if it continues to brag about the wrong stuff. But Jeremiah knows that even as late as it is, an alternative agenda for bragging is on offer, bragging that is not engaged in illusion and self-deception, but that is rooted in God's own delight.

Boast of the things that belong to God, for these are the very things that make a city work. Paul lives close to Jeremiah because they are on the same wavelength. In his theology of the cross, Paul makes a contrast not unlike that of Jeremiah:

- God's foolishness in the cross is wiser than *human wisdom;*
- God's weakness in the cross is stronger than *human strength.*

And then he finishes with Jeremiah:
Consider your call brothers and sisters:

> God chose not *the wise,* not *the strong,* not *the wealthy;*
> God chose the weak;
> God chose the foolish;
> God chose what is low and despised, things that are not.

And then finally, "Let the one who boasts, boast in the LORD."

Perhaps you are like me. Always glimpsing toward,

> *wisdom* in the ways of the world
> *might,* in controlling a little piece of the action
> *wealth,* not wealthy, but a little more

And then caught short by the teaching of Jesus

> about *steadfast love, justice, and righteousness.*

And so there we are, needing to choose, not wanting to choose, but able to choose and being offered life.

The city, every great city, that ancient one and this contemporary one, wants to brag about its successes and turn out to brag about the very matters that lead to death: wisdom, might, wealth. Imagine that this great church, and dozens like it, exist in the city to witness loud and endlessly to the city that our true ground for bragging is elsewhere:

> not the fashionable, urban agenda of wisdom, might, wealth,
> but the stuff that delights God, steadfast love, justice,
> righteousness.

The Gospel to which the church testifies in the city may be put this way: Brag! But get it right! Delight in the delights of the God of neighborly fidelity. And then brag . . . endlessly!

Central Presbyterian Church / October 19, 2002
This sermon was offered for the Janie and P. C. Enniss Lectures
on the theme of "The Church and the City."

On Reading Jeremiah 3

You evoke in us responses to your hidden rule:
　　We sing your praises,
　　We worship and adore you,
　　We give our lives over to you in gratitude—
　　　　and in obedience as we are able.

You evoke in us responses toward our neighbor;
　　Your great care for us causes us to care
　　　　for the world,
　　and we resolve to *talk the talk,*
　　　　to speak the news of your goodness,
　　　　to speak the good news of your mercy,
　　　　to speak the bad news of your impatience in
　　　　　　the face of mockery.

You evoke in us response toward our neighbor,
　　and we resolve to *walk the walk:*
　　　　not to petition your work before we have done our own
　　　　　　work
　　　　not to ask you for what we may do among ourselves . . .
　　　　　　can do . . . of mercy,
　　　　　　　　of compassion,
　　　　　　　　of forgiveness,
　　　　　　　　of peace and justice.

We mark these resolves in troubled circumstance,
　　because our talk is double-tongued,
　　because our walk is double-minded . . .

one step toward you, two steps back in fear,
one utterance toward you, two utterances reneging in
duplicity.

Given all of that—We sing your praise—
We worship and adore you—
We give our lives over to you in gratitude—
and in obedience as we are able. Amen.

June 19, 2002 (Montreat)

"Until" . . . Endlessly Enacted, Now Urgent

Psalm 73; Luke 15:11-32

Psalm 73 stands at the center of the Psalter, the first psalm of the third "book." It stands, moreover, at the center of the pietistic tradition of faith in which I have been nurtured and in which I gladly stand. I am aware that Psalm 73 does not really fit the theme of this colloquium, but this is my last chance. Besides that, Psalm 73 may be the model for all television commercials that are organized as "before" and "after," so consider this remarkable statement of faith.

I

The premise of the Psalm in v. 1 is the premise of Old Testament faith, the premise of the faith in which we stand:

> Truly God is good to Israel.

This attestation knows that God is deeply, genuinely, abidingly, reliably committed to God's people. This is the creator God who does good and gives good abundantly. This is the electing God of Exodus who has settled on this community of the beloved. This is the God of wisdom who keeps the world functioning generously. This is the God of whom the church confesses, "That all things work together for good for those who love God who are called according to his purpose" (Rom 8:28).

II

But some doubted (Matt 28:17)! Among those who doubted is this psalmist. He did not doubt out of careful reasoning. He simply found another practice of life more attractive and more compelling. He was an Israelite under Torah discipline; when he looked beyond his own rigorous practice, however, he noticed those who held Torah loosely, who got along very well indeed, without all the restraints that he had learned to take as normative. He watched them carefully . . . and envied them:

> For they have no pain;
>> their bodies are sound and sleek.
> They are not in trouble as others are;
>> they are not plagued like other people. (Ps 73:4-5)

They live very well. They are easy with casual morals; they are not worried about their neighbors; but they go from strength to strength, from party to party, from portfolio to portfolio. And out of that carefree way in the world, they become celebrities:

> Therefore the people turn and praise them,
>> and find no fault in them. (Ps 73:10)

Eventually they are so successful and so full of themselves that they scoff at the notion of a God who watches and monitors and judges. Our speaker noticed them; he disapproved of them; and then he wanted what they wanted. He wanted to be like them! He could not keep his eyes off of them. He decided to give up his Torah piety because it wasn't worth it:

> All in vain I have kept my heart clean
>> and washed my hands in innocence.
> For all day long I have been plagued,
>> and am punished every morning. (Ps 73:13-14)

I imagine this psalm to be the voice of a pastor who is required to go to church seven days a week, not treated very well or paid very well, who eventually notices how well off are those who do not live that way, who at least have free weekends! There is an aching ambivalence in this utterance when faith becomes too expensive and other ways tempt and seduce, so that faith relaxes and Torah is compromised.

III

But then, beginning at verse 18, speaks a second voice in the psalm, a contrasting voice that comes out of the same mouth. For this psalmist, like all of us, is double-minded and double-tongued. This is the "after" as I have just characterized the "before." Now the psalmist is in a new place. He is a convinced, confirmed child of the covenant, confident of Torah, glad for his identity as a child of God. He now knows, beyond a shadow of a doubt, that the mad pursuit of *commodity* by his consuming neighbors is not all it's cracked up to be. He now knows that the wild life of eager self-indulgence cannot be sustained, and even while it is sustained, it cannot bring joy or well-being. He now knows that easy living without caring much is risky. He had seen the model of life at ease and with no pain. But now, on second thought,

> Truly you set them in slippery places;
>   you make them fall to ruin.
> How they are destroyed in a moment,
>   swept away utterly by terrors! (Ps 73:18-20)

Such a life has no staying power, no gravitas, no quality of existence that one would finally envy. Such a life is a fantasy created by image-makers who readily dupe naive Torah-keepers. It cannot be sustained!

So he says, I woke up to reality, and discovered that I had been a real jerk to be attracted to that way of life. Well, not a jerk, but a "brute beast," stupid and ignorant. This psalmist reviews the slippery slope he had gone down but had stopped before his life was completely shattered, just in the nick of time.

As a rhetorical trigger concerning that other way that he now dismisses as phony, he utters his great evangelical "nevertheless":

> *Nevertheless* I am continually with you;
>   you hold my right hand.
> You guide me with your counsel,
>   and afterward you will receive me with honor.
> (Ps 73:23-24)

The psalmist has come to the judgment that while the others are in slippery places, his right hand is held by God, the God of Torah, so that he cannot slip. He now knows that this God is an adequate guide, quite in contrast to those who are sadly and destructively misguided. And then he arrives at one of the most eloquent statements of faith in all of our tradition:

Whom have I in heaven but you?
  And there is nothing on earth that I desire other than you.
My flesh and my heart may fail,
  but God is the strength of my heart and my portion forever.
  (Ps 73:25-26)

Whom indeed in heaven but you: *No one!* What on earth, but you: *Nothing! Only you,* only this God as the source and center and clue to life. He says, "God is my portion," and "portion" here means property, estate, entitlement. The speaker is clearly willing to forego all of the *commodities* of his seductive neighbors for the sake of this *communion* that is the complete fulfillment of his destiny.

His conclusion is that the very best thing is to be near God who is safe refuge and utter guarantee. The contrast between communion with God and that other tempting way of life is total and unqualified. And so, like Israel frequently does, the psalm ends in praise:

I have made the Lord God my refuge,
  to tell of all your works. (Ps 73:28b)

IV

This psalm is a rather naïve statement of the seductions and settlements of faith. It states a single either/or of *commodity* or *communion* and comes down on the side of the covenant. It echoes, surely, the teaching of Deuteronomy about the way of life and the way of death, always a chance, always a decision, and here is a model articulation of faith well embraced.

What should interest us, I imagine, is how to get from *commodity* to *communion,* for it is a travail that we and our children and our grandchildren face. Clearly our nation has become a market in which everything and everyone is reduced to a tradable commodity, and now a market embedded in an empire. It is primarily the ones "without pain" who "increase in riches" who are the war planners and the stockholders and the decision-makers—and all of us who invest in imperial "growth." Clearly the church is tempted to transpose its practice of good news in order to compete for a share of the market. And who among us does not have the simplicity of our faith made seductively complex by attractions that are shrill and loud and constant, promises of well-being and comfort and communion without the shadow of the cruciform entering in? My judgment is that the travail of the psalmist is not remote from the church, its practices, its pastors and its would-be pastors, not distant from many men and women and children who name the name, that name being enmeshed so powerfully now in a commodity enterprise.

V

At the center, the psalmist tells us how he moved from seduction to confidence, from commodity to communion. It was not an easy move:

> But when I thought how to understand this,
> > it seemed to me a wearisome task. (Ps 73:16)

It was, however, a move he made:

> until I went into the sanctuary of God;
> > then I perceived their end. (Ps 73:17)

This is the big *until* that breaks the spell of consumer ideology. This is the barbed rhetorical inconvenience that questions the magic of the market and its supportive military apparatus. This "until" is the big, jarring disruption that makes alternative life possible. "Until I went to the sanctuary." Maybe he went out of habit: "I was glad when they said unto me. . . . " But even if out of habit, this time there was a seriousness and an urgency, a wondering and a receptiveness. When he was there, in any case, it all became clear. Perhaps he was long nurtured to be ready for this flash of understanding. Or perhaps it was an abrupt new claim that came to him right out of God's holiness. In any case, the speaker arrives at a deeply new orientation. The psalmist does not tell how it happened:

- Maybe it was a mystical visionary encounter like that of Isaiah in the year that King Uzziah died. Maybe.
- But the custodian had noticed, in 1 Kgs 8:9, that there was no "presence" in the ark, only two tablets of Torah. So perhaps the "until" was only a new hearing of the commandments he had heard long ago in his family. The psalmist does not tell us, but he comes away from that moment focused and

grounded and no longer captive to the slickness of the alternative.

- Or if we transpose the "until" into Christian parlance, it is "until." The word became flesh and lived among us, and we have seen his glory, the glory as of a father's only son, full of grace and truth. (John 1:14)

We have looked into the face of Jesus and have seen the ultimate offer of communion, grace and truth, generosity and reliability that the cheap self-indulgence of the community around cannot make on its way to death.

Either way:

- *until* a vision of God in the temple, or
- *until* a re-entry into the commandments, or
- *until* seeing the face of the crucified . . .

Either way . . . until I went into the sanctuary and perceived their latter end.

VI

At the core of our faith is a gift to be received, a gift to be received in an upstream decision that contradicts the easier decisions of our culture. I judge that the church in the U.S.—in a market-driven, war-hungering, empire-thirsting environment—is at the brink of a great "until" that lets us see that the promises of this deathly ideology are indeed deathly promises, and that the alternative is the one who is endlessly our true home, our best portion, and our deep desire.

Now, I was aware that Professor Cousar would be sitting up here, so I mention this New Testament text of the Prodigal. It occurred to me that this story is Jesus' midrashic commentary on Psalm 73 in which the son plays the role of the psalmist. He is, "before," a practitioner of commodity:

Then Jesus said, "There was a man who had two sons. The younger of them said to his father, 'Father, give me the share of the property that will belong to me.'" So he divided his property between them. (Luke 15:11-12)

And he ends that scenario in a failed pursuit:

> When he had spent everything, a severe famine took place throughout that country, and he began to be in need. So he went and hired himself out to one of the citizens of that country, who sent him to his fields to feed the pigs. He would gladly have filled himself with the pods that the pigs were eating; and no one gave him anything. (Luke 15:14-16)

Then we are witnesses to his "after" when he returns home:

> So he set off and went to his father. But while he was still far off, his father saw him and was filled with compassion; he ran and put his arms around him and kissed him. Then the son said to him, "Father, I have sinned against heaven and before you; I am no longer worthy to be called your son." But the father said to his slaves, "Quickly, bring out a robe—the best one—and put it on him; put a ring on his finger and sandals on his feet. And get the fatted calf and kill it, and let us eat and celebrate; for this son of mine was dead and is alive again; he was lost and is found!" And they began to celebrate. (Luke 15:20-24)

He now is a celebrated child of the household and has come to the place where he ought to be.

But what interests us is the hidden turn of the narrative that is reported—like in Psalm 73—but also like Psalm 73, not described:

> When he came to himself. (v. 17)

What an incredible phrase! We do not know how that happened, anymore than we know how the "until" in the psalm worked. The teller of the story might have said, "Until he came to himself," because it is the same "until."

But, of course, the son does not just come "to himself." He comes to "himself" in his true identity. He comes to *himself as a beloved son* of the father. He in fact comes in his "until" to recognize that his father was the only one he wanted to be with:

> Whom have I in heaven but you?
>   And there is nothing on earth that I desire other than you.
> My flesh and my heart may fail,
>   but God is the strength of my heart and my portion
> forever. (Ps 73:25-26)

It did not matter anymore to this son that his older brother got the farm as his "portion," because the father is the son's "portion" and the only thing he wants in heaven or on earth. The son "coming to himself" is a decision grounded in the father's love that permits him to slough off his false self and become finally who he is. It is clear that in this telling Jesus fully understood the psalm. Indeed, Jesus' engagement in ministry is, among other things, that we should be weaned from the seductions of *commodity* for the gift of *communion,* a presence that leaves us in joy and well-being.

Such a poem of piety as this psalm is of course remote from our concern with the emerging world order in all of its rich complexity. Except that it is worth noting that the surge of "globalization" that besets the world church is indeed a pursuit of commodity, an overriding of local cultures in the interest of market control, and the necessary support of militarism. The world writ large is caught, as was our psalmist, as was the wayward son, in a death script. The news is that it need not be so. The news is that a powerful "until" can lead to a buoyant "nevertheless." The church, in all the complexities of globalization—and now imperialism—knows about this modest "until" and knows that everything depends upon it. Imagine that the church is the carrier of this "until" that permits well-being while the way of death and all of its terrors vanish like a phantom. We are "until" people with much to decide because we know about the "after" of life with God, our heart's true home.

Columbia Theological Seminary / April 21, 2003
Colloquium "Shaking Earth and Heaven"

On Reading Jeremiah 4

We do not live by bread alone but by your word:
    So we thank you for your word,
        that you have spoken in time of need
            with deep assurance,
        that you have spoken in times of complacency
            with deep threat,
        that you have spoken by poets bold and
            prophets daring.

So we thank you for those who have kept your word for us
    until now,
        for great editors and risk-taking priests,
        for patient copiers and diligent monks,
        for patient scribes and bold scroll-makers
            who risk their lives
            who are not always inspired but did heavy lifting
                for us,
      for fundamentalists who have known that every syllable
        needed to be kept,
        for fathers who read and studied,
        for mothers who kept scrolls safely in their aprons,
        for bishops and priests who moved into your dangerous,
           texted world.

Now we in our time put our lives always more fully
    into your word,
        to read better,
        to listen carefully,
        to turn toward your truth and away from the
           loud darkness of lies.

We hold *your word* in *our hand*,
> we are dazzled, awed, moved, disturbed,
> we are finally grateful.

We thank you for your word. Oh, and while we thank, we pray for
> bread enough for today,
>> bread for the whole community of the word,
>> bread broken . . . for today. Amen.

June 20, 2002 (Montreat)

A Resurrection Option

Micah 4:1-5 / Third Sunday in Easter

Imagine writing a poem like this one from Micah that lays out the whole future of the world on the lips of the poet:

> In the days to come . . . !

The poem pushes us who listen into the future.

- The poem is *an act of imagination* that invites us to think beyond the present, knowing that things will not stay as they are;
- The poem is *an act of hope* that portrays the future quite unlike the present, and treats the future as though it is as certain as the present;
- The poem is *an act of assurance,* that God will not stop until the world has been healed and brought to its senses;
- The poem is *an act of summons,* whereby the future is not only a gift from God but is a task for the faithful to undertake.

This poem was so crucial to the Old Testament community, because they were mired in an unbearable present tense, living under the grinding reality of one empire after another. In our time, moreover, our culture is so taken up in immediate crises of the economy and the military that there is no one left to think about God's future . . . unless it is the church.

I

There are days to come because God is Lord and therefore we must take care not to absolutize the present tense, not to freeze the moment of our fear or our triumph or our loss or our gain. The present tense is not guaranteed into the future, for God's future will endlessly put our present tense at risk.

The image of the poem is one of all the nations who will come to Jerusalem, that great city of peace. Imagine saying that about Jerusalem when the city is currently a pivot point for hatred and conflict and violence. In the days to come, Jerusalem will be Torah teacher of us all; all nations will be willing to be instructed on how to organize the future differently according to the purposes of God.

II

The key element in this instruction from Jerusalem for a viable future is that there will be *serious disarmament:*

> they shall beat their swords into plowshares,
>   and their spears into pruning hooks;
> nation shall not lift up sword against nation,
>   neither shall they learn war any more. (Mic 4:3)

The image is of people willingly dismantling their weapons, not only dismantling but transforming them into useful tools of agricultural productivity. The abandonment of weapons is not forced, but is done willingly. And if done willingly, the poem surely suggests that in time to come there will be enough trust, effective communication, and solidarity that old enemies can be a new community together.

Thus the key mark of God's future is disarmament, the transformation of the economy from a war footing to an economy of food production. Such disarmament means, every time, the capacity to yield one's fear and aggressiveness and ambition and anxiety to a larger assurance, a guarantee that we need not position ourselves for hostility because our hostility is contained in the larger intention of God for peace, justice, and well-being.

Well, of course, it is a futile exercise to utter such a poem in our military economy with all of the sloganeering and mantras of aggressive patriotism that now seem limitless among us. But then, that is always the way of a poem that tells a truth that is rooted in God's purpose and that lives close to the ground. Poets—like Micah—do not argue or engage in conventional reasoning. Rather, they glimpse and show and suggest and explode. So here stands an old, short poem in the face of war making; it announces that we get to re-choose. We are permitted a glimpse of a peaceable, peacemaking world.

Or draw it closer. Think what would happen in the church if there were disarmament among liberals and conservatives concerning the gay/lesbian issue or a dozen other such issues. Such a disarmament in the church would require confidence that our particular passions are contained in the large guarantees of God that all will be well and all will be well.

Or draw it yet closer home, and consider the ways in which our most intimate relationships in family are marked by conflict or quiet resentment or barely conceded hostility. It is promised that on all these fronts—when God's will for goodness is taken seriously—the weapons of hostility can be made into tools of productivity that enhance common life.

III

The poem of Micah suggests two conditions that are necessary for the transformation of weapons to tools for peace. The first is that there must be *lowered expectations,* the recognition that we cannot have all that we wanted in our aggressive self-assertion. The poet puts it this way:

> But they shall all sit under their own vines and under their
>   own fig trees,
> and no one shall make them afraid;
>   for the mouth of the LORD of hosts has spoken. (Mic 4:4)

The poet anticipates neighbors enjoying a very modest kind of life, one vine and one fig tree, not great vineyards or groves of fruit trees, but only one. This modesty is important on two counts. First, it is a drastic contrast to the royal sumptuousness that the urban elite in Jerusalem—in their present tense—thought they had to have in order to enjoy life. The accumulation of objects of pleasure is an endless seduction, and if one must have more and more, eventually one must usurp what belongs to someone else. Such a devouring assertiveness simply assures the practice of neighbor violence. If, however, one settles for just one vine and one fig tree, there is no need for aggressiveness or for threat to the neighbor.

The modest style of life here proposed among the peaceable is quite agrarian. This is the diet of farmer peasants who eat only what they can grow. But farmer peasants, unlike the urban elite in Jerusalem, are not the ones who make war. This verse suggests to me that we must think again about our consumer appetites that are endless in need and desire. People who care about the future as God's future must abandon such appetites and settle for modesty.

The second condition for disarmament is even more startling:

> For all the peoples walk,
>   each in the name of its god,
> but we will walk in the name of the Lord our God
>   forever and ever. (Mic 4:5)

This statement about religious loyalties proposes that the peaceable "live and let live." At the same time, the Israelites are to be clear in their devotion to their own God, but they are to give to others the freedom to walk in the name of other gods. War comes among nations, in church, and in families when we think there is *only one way* and all must conform or be coerced to conform. Peace requires giving people room for alternatives, clear on one's own commitments but open at the same time to others doing their life and faith differently. On both these conditions—lowered expectations and live and let live—peace is possible. On both counts, however, our society of military consumerism has much of which to repent.

IV

Finally, you are aware that this text is appointed for the third Sunday in Easter. This poem on this Easter Sunday surely invites us to think again about Easter. Seen through this poem, Easter is not just about our dead Lord being alive again; it is about God's capacity to work a newness in a world that has grown stale and cranky without newness. Poets tend to be open to such newness that is not argued logically or empirically, but that comes in an imaginative utterance. It is all "in the days to come." Easter Christians are those who wait for those days, and who notice that those days are already come upon us in the new life given in Christ. It is no wonder that Jesus taught, "Blessed are the peacemakers, for they will be called the children of God" (Matt 5:9). We could be children of war and resentment and fear and anxiety and aggressiveness. We need not, however, live in that way. There is another way that God intends among us, a way of peace, a more excellent way! We ourselves could be exactly children of the peace-giving God. Good news!

Grace and Holy Trinity Cathedral, Kansas City, Missouri / May 4, 2003

On Reading Jeremiah 5

We confess, gladly and boldly, that
      all our "times are in your hands." (Ps 31:15)

We affirm, with considerable relief,
     that the *NOW* of the present time, present hour, present day,
       are in your hands
       and you preside with generous sovereignty.

We affirm gladly, because we find our present *now*
       overloaded with demand,
     fraught with too much bewilderment,
     burdened with more fear than we can tolerate,
       and more pain and more anxiety,
       and more than enough of inhumanity.
    And we gladly cede our now over to you.
Even more boldly and more gladly,
      we affirm that our futures are in your hand.
         We cannot see from here to there—but you can!
You can, we affirm, see our future as a place where you will *plant*
    and we imagine you planting new community,
             new social fabric,
             new networks of well-being.
     We imagine you *building* new towers less arrogant,
             new modes of welfare and care,
             new practices of neighborliness.

You *build* and you *plant* futures that we cannot even hope:
    we say, "He is coming soon."
    we say, "Thine is the kingdom and the power and the glory."
    we say, "Amen. Come Lord Jesus." (Rev 22:20)

We gladly, boldly trust our future to you . . .
  And then we return to the reality of now, some heartened,
    a little healed,
  glad for our piece of life that we receive back from you,
    broken and poured out, our little moment of life
      abundant,
    from you with thanks, back to you in praise,
    our life, all with you, come soon. Amen.

June 21, 2002 (Montreat)

First Class in Psalms

We begin this study in a context where you
       have spoken to us in gracious, sovereign ways,
    You have spoken through prophets and apostles;
    You have spoken in Scripture that is always
       endlessly new among us;
    You have spoken among us by the
       stirring of your Spirit;
    You have spoken to us and for us in
       Jesus Christ, your word fleshed.

And now we come to answers.
We give you thanks for many mothers and many fathers
    who have responded to your utterance;
We give you thanks for songs of exuberant praise, and
       for prayers of deep trust, and
       for poems of urgent imperative, and
       for shrill fits of rage addressed to you.

In and through our study,
       break our silences,
       hear us to freedom,
       receive us in our gratitude
       and turn our bold words to thankful lives of faith and
         obedience.
       We pray through the fleshed word who is your speech
         to us,
       and our speech to you. Amen.

September 5, 2002

Index of biblical references

NEW TESTAMENT